Advanced Marriage Training For Singles By

Dr. Derrick L. Campbell

Copyright © 2014 By Derrick L. Campbell

All rights reserved. No part of this book may be reproduced in any form or by any electronic or mechanical means, including information storage and retrieval systems, without permission in writing from the publisher, except by a reviewer who may quote brief passages in a review.

All Scriptures included and referred to in the text are from the King James translation of the Holy Bible.

Published by
Derrick L. Campbell
PO Box 1668
Blackwood, New Jersey 08012
info@thepromisedlandmnistry.com
Visit our website @ www.thepromisedlandministry.com

First edition: September 2014

ISBN: 978-0-9802039-9-8

Printed in the United States of America

TABLE OF CONTENTS

	Page
Preface	v
About the Author	vii
Dedication	ix
Chapter 1. The Dysfunctional Marriage	1
Chapter 2. The Dysfunctional Organization	7
Chapter 3. The Servant Centered Marriage	11
Chapter 4. Spiritual Gifts	13
Chapter 5. The Servant Purpose	43
Chapter 6. Servant Goals	63
Chapter 7. Commands from God	107
Chapter 8. Conflict Reflection	207
Chapter 9. Commitment Analysis	217
Chapter 10. A Final Note	221
References	223

PREFACE

For several years, The Lord has blessed my wife and I to be able to facilitate marriage conferences for couples looking to enhance their marriage. As I continued, I became further concerned as to why there is such a high divorce rate. I reflected on all of the great tools and ministries around the world that improve peoples marriages. Then I asked The Lord, "Why are marriages not working". The Lord lead me to Genesis 2:15-18. The Lord revealed to me that the reason that marriages are not working is because they do not resemble His original design for marriage.

According to Genesis 2:15-18, God designed marriage with a specific purpose, path, and position. Adam's purpose was to be a servant and a steward over the resources that God provided (Genesis 2:15). Adam was provided a specific path that God gave in the form of commandments (Genesis 2:16-17). Adam was provided with a specific position in the marriage (Genesis 2:18). When any one of the three components of God's original design for marriage are dysfunctional then the probability for separation and divorce increases tremendously.

The Lord told me that I want you to share this information with people who are single. This will better equip them for marriage by helping them to make selections based on the original design for marriage and not the other superficial characteristics and values that force people to eventually contemplate divorce. Therefore, I wrote the book 'Advanced Marriage Training for Singles'.

The book - Advanced Marriage Training for Singles - comprises of several chapters. Each chapter provides a single person with activities for reflection before selecting a husband or wife. In many cases, after people have decided to marry or become engaged they do not take a closer look at the values and desires that each individual has for their marriage. It is not until after their wedding that they begin to uncover values that often contradict the values of the other person and therefore create tension in the marriage which can lead to separation or divorce.

Advanced Marriage Training for Singles begins by introducing the concepts of a dysfunctional marriage and how it is related to a dysfunctional organization. The following chapters include activities that prepare a single person for marriage before they begin the dating process or make that decision to become engaged. A single person who is better informed about themselves and their marriage expectations will select a mate that closely fits their expectations which will result in a higher level of unity between them and their future husband or wife. The book ends with chapters that provide singles with tools designed to reduce tension in their future marriage.

Writing this book required countless hours of studying the bible and research. Once God gave me this revelation, it required me to study The Word in more depth. It amazed me as to how many obstacles began to present themselves as I continued to write this book. I realized that this book is important for singles and reducing the divorce rate. I decided to just knuckle down and finish the book.

I would like to thank my wife Sheila who was instrumental in assisting me to write this book. I am thankful for her love and patience. I would also like to thank Victoria. As I continued to facilitate marriage conferences for couples, it was Victoria who insisted that if I could provide training for couples then I could provide training for singles. Thank you for your persistence Victoria.

The intended audience for this book is people who are single. While this book will help married people, people who are engaged, and people who are dating, I believe that people who have not began to officially date will benefit the most from this book. I say that because after finishing the book, the pre-dating individual will have a complete picture of their expectations and therefore make an informed decision before they begin the dating process. This will reduce the divorce rate in our country tremendously.

ABOUT THE AUTHOR

Dr. Campbell holds a Bachelor of Science degree in Electronics Engineering Technology from Capital Institute of Technology, a second Bachelor of Science degree in Math Education from the University of the District of Columbia, a Masters in Education Administration from Lincoln University, and a doctoral degree in Educational Leadership from Rowan University.

He is also the founder and CEO of DLC Consultant Group. After authoring his first book, Promoting Positive Racial Teacher-Student Classroom Relationships, in January 2008, Dr. Campbell developed a Cultural Relationship Training Program that improves teacher-student classroom relationships as well as several companion programs. He also developed the B.O.S.S. Leadership Training Program that improves manager-employee workplace relationships and relationships between Law Enforcement and their local community.

Dr. Campbell authored his second book, Leading Your Marriage into the Promised Land, in February 2009. Leading Your Marriage into the Promised Land provides advanced marriage training for couples. Following the writing of this book, he wrote two companion workbooks, one for husbands and the other for wives.

Dr. Campbell is founder and president of The Promised Land Ministry. The Promised Land Ministry provides training for churches and non-profit organizations. Churches and non-profit organizations receive training in the areas of strategic planning, team building, and leadership.

In August 2007, Dr. Campbell founded Leadership Advancement Journal which publishes articles on recent educational, organizational, and business developments that impact our culture. His articles, Reducing Cultural Bullying in Schools and Reducing Inappropriate Special Education Referrals for Historically Underserved Students, have been featured in a local New Jersey newspaper.

In November 2008, Dr. Campbell began the new Radio talk show - Culturally Speaking with Doctor Derrick. On this talk show we discussed the solutions to the cultural challenges that exist in our schools, workplaces, and community. Dr. Campbell has had a host of local and national speakers who contributed to the content of the show.

Dr. Campbell has lectured at various locations throughout the nation, including the National Association for the Advancement of Colored People (NAACP), Iron Sharpens Iron Men's Conference, and local churches. He has ministered to the youth at his home church on the topic of Christian student rights in the public schools and has ministered at another local New Jersey church on Overcoming the Poverty Cycle. He has been a board member of his church's men's ministry, Athletes United in Christ, and has participated in various church activities. He is a board member for several non-profit organizations. He has facilitated Leading Your Marriage into the Promised seminars at churches and the Iron Sharpens Iron Conference Men's Conference.

Dr. and Mrs. Campbell are available for speaking engagements.

DEDICATION

I dedicate this book to my brother who was
my lifetime playmate and friend,

Craig Alexander Campbell Sr.

RIP

February 27, 1958 to August 7, 2014

x

1

The Dysfunctional Marriage

And he answered and said unto them, "Have ye not read, that he which made them at the beginning made them male and female, And said, For this cause shall a man leave father and mother, and shall cleave to his wife: and they twain shall be one flesh? Wherefore they are no more twain, but one flesh. What therefore God hath joined together, let not man put asunder" (Matthew 19:4-6).

A marriage becomes dysfunctional when it does not operate as originally designed. God designed marriage as a union between a man and a woman. In addition, He also placed several leadership principles in the husband and wife to ensure that marriage remains functional. Figure 1 reveals that the husband leadership principles of a functional marriage are servant and stewardship. When He added the wife, He also added teamwork as the final leadership characteristics.

THE DYSFUNCTIONAL MARRIAGE

Figure 1: Functional Marriage Husband Leadership Characteristics

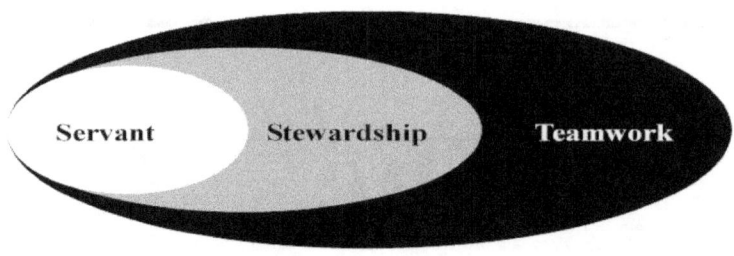

Our first example of a marriage is between Adam and Eve. God gave Adam certain responsibilities, which required certain leadership principles. When these leadership principles do not operate as God originally designed then the marriage is dysfunctional.

Genesis 2:7, records that ..."the Lord God formed man of the dust of the ground, and breathed into his nostrils the breath of life; and man became a living soul". God placed the man He created in the Garden of Eden. Then God created a habitable environment for him, which included trees that were pleasant to the sight and good for food. God placed the tree of life and the tree of the knowledge of good and evil in the Garden of Eden too. Eden also had a river that divided into four parts. God placed Adam in the Garden of Eden "... to dress it and to keep it" (Genesis 2:15).

Dressing and keeping the Garden of Eden was Adams original purpose. The word 'dress' in the Hebrew is 'abad, which means to work as a servant. The word 'keep' in the Hebrew is shamar, which means to protect. God placed Adam in the Garden of Eden to work as a servant in the garden and to protect the garden. Protecting the garden required that Adam become the steward of the garden. God granted

THE DYSFUNCTIONAL MARRIAGE

Adam stewardship over the Garden of Eden. Stewardship requires a relationship between the master and the one that the master entrusts with the resources. In this case, God is the master and He entrusted the Garden of Eden to Adam.

God provided Adam with the path that he was to follow (Genesis 2:16 - 17). God instructed Adam on what he could and could not do. At that point and time, Adam maintained his relationship with God by obeying his commands.

God decided to provide Adam with a helper. Genesis 2:18 records ..."The Lord God said, It is not good that the man should be alone; I will make him an help meet". That word 'meet' in the Hebrew is 'ezer. Ezer means to help. Eve's primary responsibility was to help Adam who was to work as a servant and to protect the Garden of Eden. The original purpose for the union between Adam and Eve was to work together as a team to serve and protect the Garden of Eden. Hence, the original purpose for the marriage between a man and a woman is to serve and protect the resources that God gives to the husband and wife through teamwork. The key for the husband is to become a servant of God so that God will provide resources for the husband to protect which will enable the wife to help with the purpose that God gives to the husband.

Noah provides an example of a husband who prospered due to his decision to become God's servants. Noah made the decision to become a servant of God and God provided him with the resources to accomplish his task that included help from his wife. Noah is the grandson of Methuselah (Genesis 5:25-29) and the son of Lamech. He was a "just man and perfect in his generation" and "walked with God" (Ezekial 14:14, 20).

During his time, the descendents of Cain and Seth began to intermarry and the result was a faction of people who were known for their ungodliness. Man's corruption increased and God decided to eliminate this wicked population from the earth (Genesis 6:7).

God entered into a covenant with Noah which guaranteed that Noah and his family would survive this judgment. God commanded that Noah build an ark (Genesis 6:14-16) and he served God's purpose by obeying Him. When Noah decided to serve God's purpose, he saved himself and his family.

THE DYSFUNCTIONAL MARRIAGE

It took Noah one hundred and twenty years to build the ark (Genesis 6:3). During that time, Noah testified to the non-believers and the wicked of that time to encourage them to repent of their evil and wicked ways. After Noah and his family finished building the ark then the "Lord shut him in" (Genesis 7:16). God flooded the earth for forty days, which resulted in the destruction of every living man, woman, and animal that remained outside of the ark.

Noah decided to become God's servant. God provided the necessary resources for Noah to complete his task. God also provided him with a wife, which provided the mechanism necessary for the team and teamwork that would accomplish the task. As a result, Noah, his wife, and his family prospered by positioning themselves to overcome the impending tragedy of God's judgment. A husband who decides to become God's servant will attain the necessary resources which includes help from his wife.

When the husband makes the decision to become God's servant, he must also make the decision to obey God. When Adam made the choice to disobey God, he also made the choice to alter the functionality of his marriage.

Adam demonstrated his disobedience in the Garden of Eden. Before God created Eve, He told Adam that he was not to eat of the tree of knowledge of good and evil (Gen. 2:17). Then God warned Adam that in the day he did eat fruit of that tree he would surely die. Shortly thereafter, Satan took on the form of a serpent (Genesis 3:1) and began to temp Eve by asking the question "Hath God not said Ye shall no eat of every tree of the garden?" Satan suggested to Eve that God was wrong with the command that he gave to Adam. Eve responded that she and Adam could eat of all the trees of the garden except the one tree called the tree of the knowledge of good and evil.

Then Satan blatantly lied and told Eve that she would not die (Genesis 3:4). Eve allowed herself to be deceived in three areas. First, Eve saw the fruit was good for food, appealing to the flesh and bodily senses. Second, she saw that it was pretty and appealed to her emotions. Finally, it appealed to her mind and intellect because she wanted to be wise (Genesis 3:6).

THE DYSFUNCTIONAL MARRIAGE

Eve failed in several areas. She refused to accept God at His Word. She doubted God, opening the door to the Devil's appeal to her flesh and her spiritual pride. She failed in her position as Adam's helper. She made the decision to disobey the instruction that God gave to Adam. She effectively disobeyed her husband Adam. She did not involve Adam in any way until after the act of disobedience was done. She became a instrument of temptation herself and offered the fruit to her husband. She failed in her role as a helper and this was the failure that became the means for Adams downfall.

Eve is not the only person that failed. According to 1 Timothy 2:14, ... "Adam was not deceived, but the woman being deceived was in the transgression". Satan's goal was to get Adam to sin by disobeying God. He used Eve's gullibility and weaker nature to get at Adam. Adam saw that Eve had eaten of the fruit, and he must have concluded that she was not dead and thus God must have lied to him too. He must have also concluded that due to the knowledge that Eve possessed that she was now wiser than him. Instead of believing God, he believed what his eyes saw and what his own wisdom concluded was real.

After Adam sinned, both their eyes were opened and they saw themselves naked and ashamed. They immediately sought to cover their nakedness and sewed fig leaves together into an apron (Genesis 3:7). God came as usual in the cool of the day to fellowship with Adam and Eve, but they tried to hide from God. Adam and Eve could not escape the presence of God, and when called, responded honestly, "...I was afraid, because I was naked; and I hid myself". (Gen. 3:10)

When questioned about how they knew that they were naked (Genesis 3:11), Adam and Eve tried to justify their actions by passing the blame. Adam, pleaded it was the fault of the woman, "...whom thou gavest to be with me" (Genesis 3:12). Adam was blaming God. As if God had not given him the woman he would not have sinned. However, Adam was not deceived as noted earlier. He with full knowledge willfully disobeyed God. Eve, followed Adam's example and said it was the serpent's fault (Genesis 3:13). "He tricked me", she said and thus she pleaded she was not responsible as well.

God judged both Adam and Eve for their transgression. God's judgment on woman was that her sorrow and conception would be multiplied (Genesis 3:16).

THE DYSFUNCTIONAL MARRIAGE

The result of sin was that the length and pain of child birth was increased. Furthermore, the woman would have a strong desire to rule over her husband. However her husband would rule over her. The same word that describes the pain of women in childbirth is used to describe man's pain in laboring for a living. The life of man would be one of hard work caused by "thorns and thistles" indicating that even the plants of earth were adversely effected by man's sin. After a hard life, man would die and be returned to the dust from which he was formed (Genesis 3:17).

The original leadership principles for man is servant and stewardship. With the addition of a woman, who becomes his wife also, include the addition of teamwork. When the husband makes the decision to disobey God by not serving in his appointment the result is a dysfunctional marriage. Couples who are in a dysfunctional marriage will also exhibit characteristics consistent with a dysfunctional organization. In my next chapter, I will discuss the characteristics of a dysfunctional organization.

2

The Dysfunctional Organization

Beloved, let us love one another: for love is of God; and every one that loveth is born of God, and knoweth God. He that loveth not knoweth not God; for God is love. In this was manifested the love of God toward us, because that God sent his only begotten Son into the world, that we might live through him. Herein is love, not that we loved God, but that he loved us, and sent his Son to be the propitiation for our sins. Beloved, if God so loved us, we ought also to love one another. No man hath seen God at any time. If we love one another, God dwelleth in us, and his love is perfected in us. Hereby know we that we dwell in him, and he in us, because he hath given us of his Spirit. And we have seen and do testify that the Father sent the Son [to be] the Saviour of the world. Whosoever shall confess that Jesus is the Son of God, God dwelleth in him, and he in God. And we have known and believed the love that God hath to us. God is love; and he that dwelleth in love dwelleth in God, and God in him (1 John 4: 7 - 16).

THE DYSFUNCTIONAL ORGANIZATION

In the previous chapter, we discussed the characteristics of a dysfunctional marriage. A dysfunctional marriage reaches that state when it does not operate as originally designed by God. God designed marriage as a union between a husband and wife that results in them becoming one flesh. When a man and woman become one flesh they become one organization.

Several scriptures, in the Holy Bible, validate that when a man and woman get married they become one organization. Adam and Eve is the first example that validates that a husband and wife form one organization.

The book of Genesis chapters one and two reveal God's greatness by Him creating heaven and earth, day and night and all of the animals. He finalized his perfection by creating man as a living soul. "The Lord God formed man of the dust of the ground, and breathed into his nostrils the breath of life; and man became a living soul" (Genesis 2:7). God then placed Adam in the Garden of Eden where he began to work. "And The Lord God took the man, and put him into the Garden of Eden to dress it and to keep it" (Genesis 2:15). After giving Adam the command to not to eat of the tree of knowledge of good and evil, "... The Lord God said , It is not good that the man should be alone; I will make him an help meet for him" (Genesis 2:18). God caused Adam to sleep and made his wife, Eve, from one of Adam's ribs.

This husband and wife union resulted in the first organization in the bible. "... Adam said, This is now bone of my bones, and flesh of my flesh; She shall be called Woman, because she was taken out of Man. Therefore shall a man leave his father and mother, and shall cleave unto his wife: and they shall be one flesh " (Genesis 2:22-23). That word flesh in the Hebrew is 'basar'. 'Basar' means person. Because of their union, Adam and Eve became one organization.

Another scripture that validates when a man and women get married that they become one is Ephesians 5:31. Ephesians 5:31 reads as follows: "For this cause shall a man leave his father and mother, and shall be joined unto his wife and they two shall be one flesh". The Greek word for flesh is 'sarx'. 'Sarx' means the body.

Even from a secular perspective, a husband and wife formulate an organization. We use the following example to prove our point.

THE DYSFUNCTIONAL ORGANIZATION

- Two people ➡ Organization
    - Two people become a pair
    - Pair is a couple
    - Couple is a team
    - Team is a group
    - Group is an organization

Two people form an organization, because two people form a pair. A pair is a couple. A couple is a team. A team is a group. Moreover, a group is an organization. Therefore, two people form an organization. Even from a secular standpoint, the husband and wife become one organization.

It is important to realize that a dysfunctional marriage is dysfunctional organization too. Dysfunctional organizations exhibit several characteristics that are detrimental to its existence. While Chris Argyris (1990) charted four factors that contribute to the dysfunctional organization, I propose that there are five different levels that contribute to a dysfunctional organization. Figure 2 reveals that the foundation for the dysfunctional organization begins with each person's use of *defense mechanisms* for coping. Defense mechanisms are the unwritten rules an individual learns and utilizes to effectively deal with circumstances that are upsetting, embarrassing, or threatening.

The second level is *skilled incompetence*, which is the outcome of the defense mechanisms we have internalized. When the defensive behaviors we've learned are transformed into a learned behavior, that behavior becomes a skill – albeit an incompetent skill – that we consider necessary in order to deal with issues that are embarrassing, threatening, or upsetting. A skill that is learned from the regular application of a defense mechanism has a high degree of incompetence embedded within it, because we are unaware of how this skill will impact our future.

Skilled incompetence transforms into a *defensive routine*. Defensive routines are the third level. When the skilled incompetence is automatically exhibited at all times, the behavior is now a defensive routine.

Defensive routines lead to *fancy footwork*. Fancy footwork is the fourth level. Fancy footwork happens when individuals try to deny the behavioral inconsistencies

THE DYSFUNCTIONAL ORGANIZATION

they exhibit, or else they place blame on other people, which results in distancing themselves from taking responsibility for their behavioral inconsistencies.

Fancy footwork leads to *organizational malaise*. Organizational malaise is the final level. During this phase the individuals in the organization – which in a church includes church leaders – will seek to find fault within the organization rather than accept responsibility for their actions and correct their behavior accordingly. The individual continues the process by accentuating the negative and deemphasizing the positive in an effort to cover up their actions. The organizational malaise is further exacerbated by a refusal of one or all the members to discuss their area of responsibility.

Figure 2.

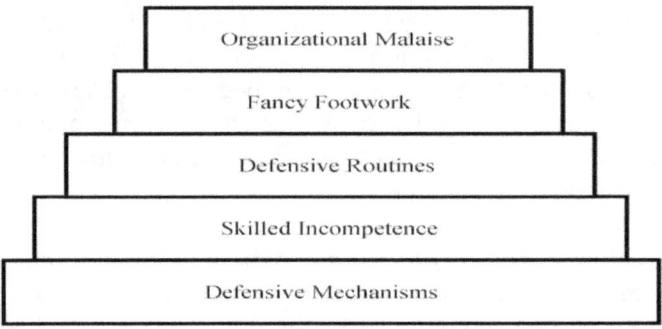

Overcoming the challenges related to a dysfunctional marriage will require that the husband embrace several leadership principles and that the wife position herself to accept the husbands area of service. In the next chapter, I will provide a process that both men and women can us to determine their purpose. This is important because it will better inform single men and women so that they can make better selections of a husband or wife.

3

The Servant Centered Marriage

As every man hath received the gift, even so minister the same one to another, as good stewards of the manifold grace of God. If any man speak, let him speak as the oracles of God; if any man minister, let him do it as of the ability which God giveth: that God in all things may be glorified through Jesus Christ, to whom be praise and dominion for ever and ever. Amen (1 Peter 4:10-11).

In chapter 1, I discussed that the first leadership principle for a successful marriage is that the man be a servant to God. God placed Adam in the Garden of Eden to dress it and keep. The first directive that God gave to Adam in the Garden of Eden was to be a servant in the purpose that I have called you to serve.

One of the major problems contributing to the dysfunctional marriage is the man's refusal to serve God where God has called him to serve. Because of the demands that our society attempts to place on men, men would rather serve their employer

THE
SERVANT CENTERED
MARRIAGE

first and then if they have time they will serve God. God does not call a man to serve man first, He calls men to serve Him first.

Even more important, woman are either satisfied with waving this requirement that the man be a servant of God or they believe that after marriage they can persuade the man to become a servant. This produces a whole set of different difficulties for the marriage.

Before the man and woman begin dating they must find their God given purpose. This will enable both the man and woman to make informed decisions regarding a potential mate. If a man knows the area that he is called to serve, he can make an informed decision regarding whether or not the potential wife can help him in the area of his calling.

If a woman knows her area to serve, she can make an informed decision as to whether or not she can help that man. Additionally, she can make a decision regarding if she is willing to submit to the man and help him in his calling and therefore sacrificing in part or whole her calling.

We begin the process for determining a persons God ordained calling with an evaluation of their Spiritual Gift. Spiritual Gifts are given to God's people by the Holy Spirit (1 Corinthians 12) to prepare people for service and for the building up of the body of Christ (Ephesians 4:12).

In the next chapter, you will identify your Spiritual Gift by completing the Spiritual Gift survey.

4

Spiritual Gifts

For I say, through the grace given unto me, to every man that is among you, not to think of himself more highly than he ought to think; but to think soberly, according as God hath dealt to every man the measure of faith. For as we have many members in one body, and all members have not the same office: So we, being many, are one body in Christ, and every one members one of another (Romans 12:3-5).

It is almost impossible for an individual to have a successful marriage without knowing their God given purpose. Each man and each woman has a purpose on this earth that glorifies the Son of God - Jesus Christ. When a man does not know his purpose, he does not know the area that he is assigned to dominate. When a woman does not know her purpose, she does not know how to help her future or perspective husband. Before a person considers marriage, they need to find their purpose so that they can unite with a spouse who has a like-minded purpose therefore increasing the probability of longevity in their marriage.

The scriptures in the New Testament of the Holy Bible assist each individual with determining their purpose. According to Romans 12, 1 Corinthians 12, Ephesians 4, and 1 Peter 4 each person has a spiritual gift to assist with their ultimate

SPIRITUAL GIFTS

purpose. Table 1 reveals the different Spiritual Gifts outlined in the New Testament.

Table 1: New Testament Spiritual Gifts			
Romans 12	1 Corinthians 12	Ephesians 4	1 Peter 4
• Prophecy • Serving • Teaching • Exhortation • Giving • Leadership • Mercy	• Word of wisdom • Word of knowledge • Faith • Gifts of healings • Miracles • Prophecy • Distinguishing between spirits • Tongues • Interpretation of tongues • Apostle • Prophet • Teacher • Miracles • Kinds of healings • Helps • Administration • Tongues	• Apostle • Prophet • Evangelist • Pastor • Teacher	• Serving • Teaching

We can begin to have a successful life in Christ when we determine our purpose, which will ultimately determines the effectiveness of our marriage. We begin this

SPIRTUAL GIFTS

process by completing the Spiritual Gift Survey. The Spiritual Gift Survey has 100 questions. There is no right or wrong responses. Each response is according to how the individual feels about the question. You answer each question by circling one of the numbers, which range from 1 to 5. A five represents that you strongly agree with the question. A four represents that you agree with the question. A three represents that you are neutral, which means that you neither agree nor disagree with the question. A two represents that you disagree. A one represents that you strongly disagree.

Let us practice before we begin. Respond to the following question:

Please Circle the number that best represents how you feel about each question.

		Strongly Agree	Agree	Neutral	Disagree	Strongly Disagree
1.	Was yesterday the best day of your life?	5	4	3	2	1

Before you begin, there are some additional directions. After you complete each response, you will transfer the value for each response to the table on pages 36-37. Then you will add the value for each row and place that total in the "Total" column. The row with the highest value will tell you what your Spiritual Gift is. After you identify your Spiritual Gift, review the Spiritual Gift Reference Chart for the meaning of your gift and the traits associated with your gift.

SPIRITUAL GIFTS
_____

Spiritual Gift Survey

Please Circle the number that best represents how you feel about each question.

		Strongly Agree	Agree	Neutral	Disagree	Strongly Disagree
1.	Would you rather do a job than find someone else to do it?	5	4	3	2	1
2.	Do your giving records show that you give more than 10% of your income to the Lord's work?	5	4	3	2	1
3.	Do you believe that when you are in charge, things seem to run smoothly?	5	4	3	2	1
4.	Do you hurt for others who are in distress, and desire to do acts of love for those who cannot or will not return them?	5	4	3	2	1
5.	Do you strongly desire to speak out boldly and directly against evil in society or in the church?	5	4	3	2	1

ADVANCED MARRIAGE TRAINING FOR SINGLES

SPIRTUAL GIFTS

Please Circle the number that best represents how you feel about each question.

		Strongly Agree	Agree	Neutral	Disagree	Strongly Disagree
6.	Does studying the Bible and sharing your insights with others for their growth in Christ seem to be very satisfying for you?	5	4	3	2	1
7.	Have you urged others to seek a biblical solution to their affliction or suffering?	5	4	3	2	1
8.	Do you have a desire to pioneer and establish new ministries or churches?	5	4	3	2	1
9.	Have you applied spiritual truth effectively to situations in your own life?	5	4	3	2	1
10.	Have others told you that you have helped them understand key and important facts of Scripture?	5	4	3	2	1

SPIRITUAL GIFTS

		Strongly Agree	Agree	Neutral	Disagree	Strongly Disagree
11.	Do you depend upon God's resources and guidance to an unusual degree?	5	4	3	2	1
12.	Are you sometimes prophetic when exercising an interpretation of tongues for the church?	5	4	3	2	1
13.	Do you experience an intimacy with God which inspires you to serve and edify others?	5	4	3	2	1
14.	Can you judge between the inadequate and the acceptable, or between evil and good?	5	4	3	2	1
15.	Do you enjoy handling the details of organizing ideas, people, resources and time for a more effective ministry?	5	4	3	2	1

SPIRTUAL GIFTS

		Strongly Agree	Agree	Neutral	Disagree	Strongly Disagree
16.	When you do things behind the scenes and others are helped, are you joyful and do not care who gets the credit?	5	4	3	2	1
17.	Have others told you that God healed them of an emotional problem when you ministered to them?	5	4	3	2	1
18.	Does God seem to regularly do impossible things through your life?	5	4	3	2	1
19.	Do you enjoy sharing the gospel?	5	4	3	2	1
20.	Have you helped individual believers, over a period of time, by guiding them to relevant portions of the Bible and praying with them?	5	4	3	2	1

SPIRITUAL GIFTS

		Strongly Agree	Agree	Neutral	Disagree	Strongly Disagree
21.	Do you sense God's purpose and pleasure in meeting every day responsibilities?	5	4	3	2	1
22.	When you are moved by an appeal to give to God's work, do you usually find the money you need to respond?	5	4	3	2	1
23.	Do you find it easy to motivate others to follow through on a ministry project?	5	4	3	2	1
24.	Have you cared for others when they have had material or physical needs?	5	4	3	2	1
25.	Do you sometimes have a strong sense of what God wants to say to people in response to a particular situation?	5	4	3	2	1

SPIRTUAL GIFTS

		Strongly Agree	Agree	Neutral	Disagree	Strongly Disagree
26.	Have people told you that you have helped them learn biblical truth in a meaningful way?	5	4	3	2	1
27.	Do you have a desire to effectively counsel the perplexed, the guilty, or the addicted?	5	4	3	2	1
28.	Do you have the ability to adapt to different surroundings by being culturally sensitive and aware?	5	4	3	2	1
29.	Can you intuitively arrive at solutions to complicated problems?	5	4	3	2	1
30.	Do you enjoy studying and reading quite a bit in order to learn biblical truths?	5	4	3	2	1

SPIRITUAL GIFTS

		Strongly Agree	Agree	Neutral	Disagree	Strongly Disagree
31.	Have there been times when you have felt sure you knew God's specific will for the future growth of His work, even when others have not been so sure?	5	4	3	2	1
32.	Do you understand an unlearned language and communicate that message to the body of Christ?	5	4	3	2	1
33.	Do you worship the Lord with unknown words too deep for the mind to comprehend?	5	4	3	2	1
34.	Are you given affirmation by other Christians that you are able to distinguish spiritual untruth from supernatural insights?	5	4	3	2	1
35.	Are you able to give directions to others without using persuasion to get them to accomplish a task?	5	4	3	2	1

SPIRTUAL GIFTS

		Strongly Agree	Agree	Neutral	Disagree	Strongly Disagree
36.	Have other Christians told you that you have helped them become more effective in their ministries?	5	4	3	2	1
37.	Has physical healing occurred because of your praying for people?	5	4	3	2	1
38.	Can others point to specific instances when your prayers have resulted in visible miracles?	5	4	3	2	1
39.	Have you led others to Christ?	5	4	3	2	1
40.	Is it your desire to commit yourself sacrificially to care for the spiritual welfare of a group of young Christians? Shut-ins? Or people in pain?	5	4	3	2	1

SPIRITUAL GIFTS

		Strongly Agree	Agree	Neutral	Disagree	Strongly Disagree
41.	Do you enjoy knowing that you are freeing up others to do what God has called them to do?	5	4	3	2	1
42.	Do you believe that God will meet your needs as long as you give to Him sacrificially and consistently?	5	4	3	2	1
43.	Do you believe that when you join a group, others expect you to take the leadership?	5	4	3	2	1
44.	Do you work joyfully with and help those people who are ignored by the majority of those around them?	5	4	3	2	1
45.	Has God enabled you to reveal specific things that will happen in the future?	5	4	3	2	1

SPIRTUAL GIFTS

		Strongly Agree	Agree	Neutral	Disagree	Strongly Disagree
46.	Do you enjoy giving considerable time to learning biblical truth in order to minister to children and/or adults?	5	4	3	2	1
47.	Have people come to you in their afflictions or sufferings, and told you that they have been helped, relieved, and healed by you?	5	4	3	2	1
48.	Do you have a desire to minister to people in other communities or countries?	5	4	3	2	1
49.	Have people indicated that you have perceived and applied Biblical truths to their specific needs?	5	4	3	2	1
50.	Have you frequently discovered new insights into Scripture through personal study?	5	4	3	2	1

SPIRITUAL GIFTS

		Strongly Agree	Agree	Neutral	Disagree	Strongly Disagree
51.	Have other people told you that you have the faith to accomplish what seemed impossible to them?	5	4	3	2	1
52.	Do you edify the Body by interpreting a timely message from God?	5	4	3	2	1
53.	Do you speak in a language you have never learned or do not understand?	5	4	3	2	1
54.	Have others in the church noted that you are able to see through phoniness before it is evident to other people?	5	4	3	2	1
55.	Do you enjoy bearing the responsibility for the success of a particular task within the church?	5	4	3	2	1

SPIRTUAL GIFTS

		Strongly Agree	Agree	Neutral	Disagree	Strongly Disagree
56.	Have you assisted Christian leaders to relieve them for their essential job?	5	4	3	2	1
57.	When you pray for the sick, either you or they feel sensations of tingling or warmth.	5	4	3	2	1
58.	Have people told you that The Lord used you to bring supernatural change in their lives or circumstances?	5	4	3	2	1
59.	Are you at ease in sharing how Christ has changed your life?	5	4	3	2	1
60.	Would you be concerned about guarding, like a shepherd, a group of Christian sheep from those who are "wolves," i.e., enemies of Christians?	5	4	3	2	1

SPIRITUAL GIFTS

		Strongly Agree	Agree	Neutral	Disagree	Strongly Disagree
61.	Do you respond cheerfully when asked to do a job, even if it seems menial?	5	4	3	2	1
62.	Do you seek to manage your money well in order to give liberally to the Lord's work?	5	4	3	2	1
63.	Do you believe that when you set goals, others seem to accept them readily?	5	4	3	2	1
64.	Would you enjoy spending time with a lonely, shut-in person or someone in prison?	5	4	3	2	1
65.	Do you strongly desire to speak direct messages from God that edify, exhort, or comfort others?	5	4	3	2	1

SPIRTUAL GIFTS

		Strongly Agree	Agree	Neutral	Disagree	Strongly Disagree
66.	When you communicate biblical truth to others, do you see changes in knowledge, attitudes, values, or conduct?	5	4	3	2	1
67.	Can you effectively motivate people to get involved in ministry when such motivation is needed?	5	4	3	2	1
68.	Do you have a unique ability to give helpful leadership to several churches?	5	4	3	2	1
69.	Have you sensed God's presence and direction when important decisions needed to be made?	5	4	3	2	1
70.	Do you enjoy doing word studies, examining the historical background of a text, and getting at the facts of a passage in order to benefit yourself and other believers?	5	4	3	2	1

SPIRITUAL GIFTS

		Strongly Agree	Agree	Neutral	Disagree	Strongly Disagree
71.	Have you believed God for the impossible and seen it happen in a tangible way?	5	4	3	2	1
72.	Do you glorify God and demonstrate his power through this miraculous manifestation?	5	4	3	2	1
73.	Do you communicate a message given by God for the church?	5	4	3	2	1
74.	Are you able to differentiate between demonic influence and mental illness?	5	4	3	2	1
75.	Have you ever made effective and efficient plans for accomplishing the goals of a group?	5	4	3	2	1

SPIRTUAL GIFTS

		Strongly Agree	Agree	Neutral	Disagree	Strongly Disagree
76.	Would you rather be a supportive background person than an up-front leader or speaker?	5	4	3	2	1
77.	Have you been used to cure diseases instantly, in the name of The Lord?	5	4	3	2	1
78.	Are you able to change circumstances through the name of The Lord?	5	4	3	2	1
79.	Do you wish to relate to non-Christians so you can share your faith?	5	4	3	2	1
80.	Do you enjoy relating to a certain group of people in long-term relationships, sharing personally in their successes and failures as well as assuming responsibility for their spiritual well-being?	5	4	3	2	1

SPIRITUAL GIFTS

		Strongly Agree	Agree	Neutral	Disagree	Strongly disagree
81.	Do you attach spiritual value to practical service?	5	4	3	2	1
82.	Are you willing to maintain a lower standard of living in order to benefit God's work?	5	4	3	2	1
83.	When you speak, do people seem to listen and agree?	5	4	3	2	1
84.	Do you enjoy visiting in hospitals and/or nursing homes, and feel you do well in such a ministry?	5	4	3	2	1
85.	Have people told you that you have communicated timely and urgent messages, which must have come directly from the Lord?	5	4	3	2	1

SPIRTUAL GIFTS

		Strongly Agree	Agree	Neutral	Disagree	Strongly Disagree
86.	Can you make difficult biblical truths understandable to others?	5	4	3	2	1
87.	Have you verbally encouraged the wavering, the troubled, or the discouraged?	5	4	3	2	1
88.	Do you demonstrate authority and vision for the mission of the church?	5	4	3	2	1
89.	Do others ask you for workable ideas or alternatives?	5	4	3	2	1
90.	Do you long to share with others the biblical insights that you discover?	5	4	3	2	1

SPIRITUAL GIFTS

		Strongly Agree	Agree	Neutral	Disagree	Strongly Disagree
91.	When you are in a group, are you the person others often look to for vision?	5	4	3	2	1
92.	Do you respond to a message spoken in tongues by giving an interpretation?	5	4	3	2	1
93.	Do you express with an interpretation a word by the Spirit, which edifies the church?	5	4	3	2	1
94.	Is your determination that the person who is teaching is from God, Satan, or of human origin later confirmed to be true?	5	4	3	2	1
95.	If a group you are in is lacking organization, do you desire to step in to help it run more smoothly?	5	4	3	2	1

SPIRTUAL GIFTS

		Strongly Agree	Agree	Neutral	Disagree	Strongly Disagree
96.	Do you enjoy doing routine tasks that lead to more effective ministry by others?	5	4	3	2	1
97.	Do you enjoy praying for sick people because you know that some of them will be healed as a result?	5	4	3	2	1
98.	Has God asked you to perform supernatural signs and wonders?	5	4	3	2	1
99.	Do unbelievers understand you when you explain who Christ is and how to become a Christian?	5	4	3	2	1
100.	Are you able to feed followers in Christ by guiding them through selected Bible passages?	5	4	3	2	1

SPIRITUAL GIFTS

In the table below, enter the numerical value for each of your responses next to the number of the corresponding statement from **STEP I**. Then add up the five numbers that you have recorded in each row and place the sum in the "Total" column.

Value of Answers					Total	Gift
1= ____	21= ____	41= ____	61= ____	81= ____		Serving
2= ____	22= ____	42= ____	62= ____	82= ____		Giving
3= ____	23= ____	43= ____	63= ____	83= ____		Leading
4= ____	24= ____	44= ____	64= ____	84= ____		Mercy
5= ____	25= ____	45= ____	65= ____	85= ____		Prophecy
6= ____	26= ____	46= ____	66= ____	86= ____		Teaching
7= ____	27= ____	47= ____	67= ____	87= ____		Exhortation
8= ____	28= ____	48= ____	68= ____	88= ____		Apostle
9= ____	29= ____	49= ____	69= ____	89= ____		Wisdom
10= ____	30= ____	50= ____	70= ____	90= ____		Knowledge

SPIRTUAL GIFTS

Value of Answers					Total	Gift
11= ___	31= ___	51= ___	71= ___	91= ___		Faith
12= ___	32= ___	52= ___	72= ___	92= ___		Interpretation
13= ___	33= ___	53= ___	73= ___	93= ___		Tongues
14= ___	34= ___	54= ___	74= ___	94= ___		Discerning
15= ___	35= ___	55= ___	75= ___	95= ___		Administration
16= ___	36= ___	56= ___	76= ___	96= ___		Helps
17= ___	37= ___	57= ___	77= ___	97= ___		Healing
18= ___	38= ___	58= ___	78= ___	98= ___		Miracles
19= ___	39= ___	59= ___	79= ___	99= ___		Evangelist
20= ___	40= ___	60= ___	80= ___	100= ___		Pastor

SPIRITUAL GIFTS

Spiritual Gift Reference Chart

Spiritual Gift	Definition	Scriptural References	Traits
Administration	The gift of Administration is the divine enablement to understand what makes an organization function, and the special ability to plan and execute procedures that accomplish the goals of the ministry.	1 Cor. 12:28	- Thorough - Objective - Responsible - Organized - Goal-oriented - Efficient - Conscientious
Apostle	The gift of Apostleship is the divine ability to start and oversee the development of new churches or ministry structures.	1 Cor. 12:28,29 Eph 4:11-12	- Adventurous - Entrepreneurial - Persevering - Adaptable - Culturally sensitive - Risk-taking - Cause-drive
Discernment	The gift of Discernment is the divine enablement to distinguish between truth and error. It is able to discern the spirits, differentiation between good and evil, right and wrong.	1 Cor. 12:10	- Perceptive - Insightful - Sensitive - Intuitive - Decisive - Challenging - Truthful

SPIRTUAL GIFTS

Spiritual Gift	Definition	Scriptural References	Traits
Exhortation	The gift of Encouragement is the divine enablement to present truth, so as to strengthen, comfort, or urge to action those who are discouraged or wavering in their faith.	Romans 12:8	• Positive • Motivating • Challenging • Affirming • Reassuring • Supportive • Trustworthy
Evangelism	The gift of Evangelism is the divine enablement to effectively communicate the gospel to unbelievers so they respond in faith and move toward discipleship.	Eph. 4:11	• Sincere • Candid • Respected • Influential • Spiritual • Confident • Commitment-oriented
Faith	The gift of Faith is the divine enablement to act on God's promises with confidence and unwavering belief in God's ability to fulfill His purposes.	1 Cor. 12:9	• Prayerful • Optimistic • Trusting • Assured • Positive • Inspiring • Hopeful
Giving	The gift of Giving is the divine enablement to contribute money and resources to the work of the Lord with cheerfulness and liberality. People with this gift do not ask, "How much money do I need to give God?" But, "How much money do I need to live on?"	Romans 12:8	• Stewardship-oriented • Responsible • Charitable • Trust in God • Disciplined

SPIRITUAL GIFTS

Spiritual Gift	Definition	Scriptural References	Traits
Healing	The gift of Healing is the divine enablement to pray in faith specifically for people who need physical, emotional, or spiritual healing.	1 Cor. 12:9; 28,30	• Compassionate • Trust in God • Prayerful • Full of Faith • Humble • Responsive • Obedient
Helps	The gift of Helps is the divine enablement to accomplish practical and necessary tasks which free-up, support, and meet the needs of others.	1 Cor. 12:28 Rom. 12:7	• Available • Willing • Helpful • Reliable • Loyal • Dependable • Whatever-it-takes attitude
Interpretation	The gift of Interpretation is the divine enablement to make known the message of one who speaks in tongues.	1 Cor. 12:10	• Worshipful • Responsive • Devoted • Responsible • Spiritually intimate • Sensitive • Faithful
Knowledge	The gift of Knowledge is the divine enablement to bring truth to the Body of Christ through a revelation or Biblical insight.	1 Cor. 12:8	• Inquisitive • Responsive • Observant • Insightful • Reflective • Studious • Truthful
Leadership	The gift of Leadership is the divine enablement to cast vision, motivate, and direct people to harmoniously accomplish the purposes of God.	Rom. 12:8	• Influential • Diligent • Visionary • Trustworthy • Persuasive • Motivating • Goal-setter

SPIRTUAL GIFTS

Spiritual Gift	Definition	Scriptural References	Traits
Mercy	The Mercy gift is the divine enablement to cheerfully and practically help those who are suffering or are in need, compassion moved to action.	Rom. 12:8	• Empathetic • Caring • Kind • Sensitive • Burden-bearing • Responsive
Miracles	The gift of miracles is the divine enablement to serve as human agents thorough whom it pleases God to perform powerful acts that are perceived by observers to have altered the ordinary course of nature.	1 Cor. 12:10, 28-29	• Bold • Venturesome • Authoritative • God-fearing • Convincing • Prayerful • Responsive
Prophecy	The gift of Prophecy is the divine enablement to reveal truth and proclaim it in a timely and relevant manner for understanding, correction, repentance, or edification. There may be immediate or future implications.	Rom. 12:6 1 Cor. 12:10,28	• Discerning • Compelling • Uncompromising • Outspoken • Authoritative • Convicting • Confronting
Serving	The gift of serving is the divine enablement to identify the unmet needs involved in a task related to God's work, and to make use of available resources to meet those needs and help accomplish the desired goals.	Rom. 12:6-7	• Practical • Humble • Supportive • Adaptable • Responsive • Diligent • Observant
Shepherding/ Pastoring	The gift of Shepherding/Pastoring is the divine enablement to nurture, care for, and guide people toward on-going spiritual maturity and becoming like Christ.	Eph. 4:11,12	• Influencing • Nurturing • Guiding • Disciplining • Protective • Supportive • Relational

SPIRITUAL GIFTS

Spiritual Gift	Definition	Scriptural References	Traits
Teaching	The gift of Teaching is the divine enablement to understand, clearly explain, and apply the Word of God, causing greater Christ-likeness in the lives of listeners.	1 Cor. 12:28, 29	• Disciplined • Perceptive • Teachable • Authoritative • Practical • Analytical • Articulate
Tongues	The gift of Tongues is the divine enablement to receive a spontaneous message from God in public worship and t speak it in an unknown language that is then made know to the church through the gift of interpretation.	1 Cor. 12:10, 28-30	• Worshipful • Prayerful • Trusting • Devoted • Spontaneous • Receptive
Wisdom	The gift of Wisdom is the divine enablement to apply spiritual truth effectively to meet a need in a specific situation.	1 Cor. 12:8	• Sensible • Insightful • Practical • Wise • Fair • Experienced • Common Sense

You have successfully identified your Spiritual Gift(s). In some cases, you may find that you have more than one dominant Spiritual Gift. In that case, review the Spiritual Gift traits and identify the Spiritual Gift that you believe is the most dominate. In the next chapter, you will use your Spiritual Gift evaluation to help to determine your servant purpose.

5

The Servant Purpose

But Jesus called them to him, and saith unto them, Ye know that they which are accounted to rule over the Gentiles exercise lordship over them; and their great ones exercise authority upon them. But so shall it not be among you: but whosoever will be great among you, shall be your minister: And whosoever of you will be the chiefest, shall be servant of all. For even the Son of man came not to be ministered unto, but to minister, and to give his life a ransom for many (Mark 10:42-45).

Your personal vision forms the cornerstone for your existence. When a husband and wife have a like-minded vision then they can expect a marriage full of joy and happiness. To explain this concept we can use a rubber band. If you take the rubber band and stretch it, you will create tension in the rubber band. If you stretch, the rubber band to a great extreme the rubber band will break. If you do not stretch the rubber band, the rubber band will not break. This is what happens when two people get married with extreme opposite visions for their life. As time continues to move on, the tension between the two visions, continues to stretch until the marriage breaks. Furthermore, when the two visions exhibit no tension the marriage will never break. And if the two visions are the same, then nothing will ever become between the husband and wife.

THE SERVANT PURPOSE

Aquila and Priscilla provide a biblical example of a couple who had the same vision. This couple was determined to labor together to serve Christ. Their names appear six times in the bible (Acts 18:2,18,26; Romans 16:3, 1 Corinthians 16:19, 2 Timothy 4:19). The Apostle Paul was attracted to this couple, which means that they had serving our Lord and Savoir - Jesus Christ - as their primary focus. Both Paul and the couple were involved in the tent making business too (Acts 18:3).

After ministering in Corinthian, Paul decided to continue his efforts in Ephesus. Aquila and Priscilla accompanied Paul and established a church in their home (1 Corinthians 16:19). While in Ephesus, they encountered Apollos, a Jewish preacher from Alexandria (Egypt) who was eloquent and mighty in the Scriptures, but he only knew of the baptism of John (Acts 18:24-25). After the meeting, they took Apollos to their home, and explained to him the finer points of The Word of God and his salvation (Acts 18:26). The next time that the scriptures mention Aquila and Priscilla they are back in Rome (Romans 16:3-5). Finally, the scriptures mention them in Ephesus again (2 Timothy 4:19).

The scriptures always mention the couple's names together. This is an indication of not only their allegiance to Christ but also their allegiance to one another. This couple was connected to one another spiritually, in business, and intellectually. Their spiritually connectedness is evidenced by living lives centered on The Lord and His Church. Their business connectedness is apparent because they worked together as tent makers. Finally, their intellectual connectedness is evidenced by their knowledge of sharing the scriptures with others.

It is important that individuals determine their personal vision before seeking marriage. When a man knows his personal vision, then he knows what to seek for in a wife. When a woman knows her personal vision, she knows if she is suitable to help the husband.

THE SERVANT PURPOSE

You began the personal vision development process by determining your Spiritual Gift. Follow the following guidelines to complete the process.

1. Refer to the example on pages 46-47.
2. Complete the chart on page 48.
3. Complete the Things I really Enjoy Doing When Using My Spiritual Gift column. Since you have identified your dominant Spiritual Gift, list three of the traits that are found in the Spiritual Gift Reference Chart on pages 38 - 42.
4. Complete the What Brings Me Happiness/Joy When Using My Spiritual Gift column. Think about what brings you happiness when using your Spiritual Gift. Write this in the What Brings Me Happiness/Joy When Using My Spiritual Gift column.
5. Complete The Two Best Moments of My Past Week When Using My Spiritual Gift column. If needed, refer to the definitions of each Spiritual Gift in the previous chapter.
6. Complete the Three Ministries That I Would Work in If I No Longer Had to Work column. Refer to the ministry list on page 51 for hints. This list is not inclusive. Add other ministries to your column if needed.
7. Complete the Issues and Causes I Care About Deeply column. Think about three issues or causes that you care the most about. Write them in the column.
8. Complete the My Most Important Values column. Refer to the Kingdom of Heaven Character Chart on pages 52 - 61 for hints regarding My Most Important Values.
9. Complete the Things I Can Do at the Good-to-Excellent Level when Using My Spiritual Gift column. Refer to the definitions for the Spiritual Gifts for hints regarding Things I Can Do at the Good-to-Excellent Level when Using My Spiritual Gift.
10. Complete the What I'd Like to Help People to Stop Doing or Do as Little as Possible column. Refer to the Issues and Causes I Care About Deeply column for hints.
11. Complete the Personal Vision Statement by filling in the blank.
12. Rewrite your vision if necessary.

THE SERVANT PURPOSE

Things I Really Enjoy Doing When Using My Spiritual Gift	What Brings Me Happiness/Joy When Using My Spiritual Gift	The Two Best Moments in the Past When Using My Spiritual Gift	Three Ministries That I would Serve In If I No Longer had to Work For A Living
Risk Taking Entrepreneur Cause-driven Adventurous	Knowing that I am serving my purpose	Overcame a church split Helped men enhance their marriages	Entrepreneur Men Marriage
Issues or Causes I Care Deeply About	**My Most Important Values**	**Things I Can Do at the Good-to-Excellent Level When Using My Spiritual Gift**	**What I'd Like to Help People to Stop Doing or Do as Little as Possible**
Unity in the family Unity in the church	Fairness Honesty Integrity	Team building	Separation in the family Separation in the church

**THE
SERVANT
PURPOSE**

My vision is to serve with **fairness, honesty, and integrity** in the
                                        (Most Important Values)

    Men's ministry by using   **team building**   to bring
  (Ministry Name)   (Good-to-Excellent Level)

unity in the family so that there no longer exists
  (Issues or Causes)

separation in the family.
    (Stop Doing)

THE SERVANT PURPOSE

Things I Really Enjoy Doing When Using My Spiritual Gift	What Brings Me Happiness/Joy When Using My Spiritual Gift	The Two Best Moments of My Past Week When Using My Spiritual Gift	Three Ministries That I would Serve In If I No Longer had to Work For A Living
Issues or Causes I Care Deeply About	**My Most Important Values**	**Things I Can Do at the Good-to-Excellent Level When Using My Spiritual Gift**	**What I'd Like to Help People to Stop Doing or Do as Little as Possible**

THE
SERVANT
PURPOSE

Personal Vision Statement

1. Based on your responses, fill in the blanks to begin writing your personal vision for serving God:

My vision is to serve with _____ in
(Most Important Values)

the _____ ministry by using _____ to
(Ministry Name)   (Good-to-Excellent Level)

bring _____ so that there no
(Issues or Causes)

longer exists _____.
(Stop Doing)

**THE
SERVANT
PURPOSE**

Personal Vision Statement

2. Rewrite and revise you vision below:

_____
_____
_____
_____
_____
_____
_____

THE SERVANT PURPOSE

Ministry Service Area Chart

☐	Academic	☐	Facility/Grounds	☐	Prayer
☐	Administration	☐	Finance	☐	Prison
☐	Aerobics	☐	Fitness	☐	Public Relations
☐	Announcement	☐	Foster Care	☐	Radio
☐	Audio	☐	Golf	☐	Recreation
☐	Baptismal Preparation	☐	Grandparents	☐	Scholarship
☐	Basketball	☐	Greeters	☐	Security
☐	Benevolent	☐	Health	☐	Singles
☐	Bereavement	☐	Hospitality	☐	Sports
☐	Bookstore	☐	Kitchen	☐	Television
☐	Bowling	☐	Landscaping	☐	Tutoring
☐	Building Committee	☐	Legal	☐	Transportation
☐	Catering	☐	Marriage	☐	Trustee
☐	Children	☐	Media	☐	Ushers
☐	Christian Education	☐	Men's Day	☐	Van
☐	Custodial Maintenance	☐	Men	☐	Web Site
☐	Dance	☐	Missions	☐	Wedding
☐	Daycare	☐	Motorcycle	☐	Young Adult
☐	Deacon	☐	Music	☐	Youth
☐	Domestic Violence	☐	Parking Lot	☐	Video
☐	Drama	☐	Pastor's Care	☐	Other_____
☐	Entrepreneur	☐	Praise and Worship		

Note: The Listing is not inclusive. Pleas add additional ministries as needed.

THE SERVANT PURPOSE

Kingdom of Heaven Character Traits

Character Traits	Definition	Bible Verse
Appreciation	Giving God our heartfelt thanks as a lifestyle of worship and adoration. This allows us to give to and value others with respect.	Rom. 12:10
Alertness	Being aware of the physical and spiritual events taking place around you so that you can have the right responses to them.	Mark 14:28
Attentiveness	Showing the worth of a person by giving undivided attention to his words and emotions.	Heb. 2:1
Availability	Adjusting your personal responsibilities around the needs of those whom I am serving.	Phil. 2:20
Boldness	Confidence that what I have to say or do is true and right and just in the sight of God.	Acts 4:29
Caution	Knowing how important right timing is in accomplishing right actions.	Pro. 19:2

THE SERVANT PURPOSE

Character Traits	Definition	Bible Verse
Confidence	Relying on the Lord for all things in our life.	Phil. 4:13
Contentment	Realizing God has provided everything I need for my present happiness.	1 Tim. 6:8
Conviction	Devotion to and following of the precepts of Scripture with zeal, whatever the cost.	Dan. 1:8
Courage	Realizing that God has given us the strength to face any situation, trial, or peril.	Deut. 31:6
Creativity	Applying God's wisdom and practical insights to a need or task.	Rom. 12:2
Decisiveness	The ability to finalize difficult decisions based on the will and ways of God.	Jam. 1:5
Deference	Limiting my freedom to speak and act in order not to offend the taste of others.	Rom. 14:21

THE SERVANT PURPOSE

Character Traits	Definition	Bible Verse
Dependability	Fulfilling what I consented to do even if it means unexpected sacrifice.	Psa. 15:4
Determination	Purposing to accomplish God's goals in God's timing regardless of the opposition.	2 Tim. 4:7-8
Devotion	Aligning personal desires, plans, worship, and hope with God.	Col. 3:2
Diligence	Visualizing each task as a special assignment from the Lord and using all my energies to accomplish it.	Col. 3:23
Discernment	The God-given ability to understand why things happen to others and to me.	1 Sam. 16:7
Discretion	The ability to avoid words, actions, and attitudes which could result in undesirable consequences.	Pro. 22:3
Endurance	The inward strength to withstand the stress to accomplish God's best.	Gal. 6:9

THE SERVANT PURPOSE

Character Traits	Definition	Bible Verse
Enthusiasm	Expressing with my spirit the joy of my soul.	1 Thes. 5:15-16
Fairness	Sees a situation from the viewpoint of each person involved and not just ours.	Mat. 7:12
Faith	Visualizing what God intends to do in a given situation and acting in harmony with it.	Heb. 11:1
Flexibility	Not setting my affections on ideas or plans, which could be changed by God or others.	Col. 3:2
Forgiveness	Clearing the record of those who have wronged me and me allowing God to love them through me.	Eph. 4:32
Generosity	Realizing that all I have belongs to God and using it for His purposes.	2 Cor. 9:6
Gentleness	Showing personal care and concern in meeting the needs of others.	1 Thes. 2:7
Gratitude	Making known to God and others in what ways they have benefited my life.	1 Cor. 4:7

THE SERVANT PURPOSE

Character Traits	Definition	Bible Verse
Honesty	Being truthful and doing what is sincere and right before God and others.	Heb. 7:26
Hospitality	Cheerfully sharing food, shelter, and spiritual refreshment with those whom God brings into my life.	Heb. 13:2
Humility	Seeing the contrast between God's holiness and my sinfulness.	Jam. 4:6
Integrity	Obedience to a moral code of values that have honor, truth, and reliability.	Psa. 78:72
Initiative	Recognizing and doing what needs to be done before I am asked to do it.	Rom. 12:21
Joyfulness	The result of knowing that God is perfecting life in others through me.	Pro. 15:13
Just	Doing what is fair, moral, impartial, and right, according to God's will.	Gen. 6:9

THE SERVANT PURPOSE

Character Traits	Definition	Bible Verse
Justice	Personal responsibility to God's unchanging laws.	Mic. 6:8
Kindness	Practicing benevolence and a loving attitude towards others.	Eph. 4:32
Love	Giving to others' basic needs without having personal rewards as my motive.	1 Cor. 13:3
Loyalty	Using difficult times to demonstrate my commitment to God and to those whom he has called me to serve.	John 15:13
Meekness	Yielding my personal rights and expectations to God.	Psa. 62:5
Obedience	Fulfilling instructions so that God and the one I am serving will fully be satisfied.	2 Cor. 10:5
Orderliness	Arranging my life and surrounding so that God has maximum freedom to achieve His goals through me.	1 Cor. 14:40
Optimism	Thinking the best of and being positive with people and all situations, even if later proven wrong.	John 16:33

THE
SERVANT
PURPOSE

Character Traits	Definition	Bible Verse
Patience	Accepting a difficult situation from God without giving Him a deadline to remove it.	Rom. 5:34
Peace	Surrendering and yielding to the Lord's control.	Phil. 4:7
Perseverance	Not being faint with our call, but being able to persist and continue to deal with stress so we can accomplish what God calls us to.	Gal. 6:9
Persuasiveness	Using words, which cause the listener's spirit to conform that he is hearing truth.	2 Tim. 2:24
Prudence	Implementing and applying good, logical, and just judgment to situations that will help in avoiding error and problems.	Pro. 13:6
Punctuality	Showing respect for other people and the limited time that God has given to them.	Ecc. 3:1
Purpose	Knowing who we are in Christ and acting it out with our call.	John 15

THE SERVANT PURPOSE

Character Traits	Definition	Bible Verse
Resourcefulness	Wise use of that which others would normally overlook or discard.	Luke 16:10
Respect	Being polite and courteous to the people, and the civil authorities God has placed in our life.	1 Thes. 5:13
Responsibility	Knowing and doing what God and others are expecting from you.	Rom. 14:12
Reverence	Awareness of how God is working through the people and events in my life to produce the character of Christ in me.	Pro. 23:17
Security	Structuring my life around what is eternal and cannot be destroyed or taken away.	John 6:27
Self-control	Instant obedience to the initial prompting of God's Spirit.	Gal. 5:24-25
Sensitivity	Knowing by the prompting of God's Spirit what words and actions will benefit the lives of others.	Rom. 12:15
Sincerity	Eagerness to do what is right with transparent motives.	1 Pet. 1:22

THE SERVANT PURPOSE

Character Traits	Definition	Bible Verse
Submission	Surrendering and yielding our will and plans over to God's guidance.	Eph. 5:21
Tact	Being considerate, delicate, and diplomatic with other's feelings and ideas, doing, and saying the right thing.	Col. 4:6
Temperance	Having self-control so we do not lose control and give in to lust and extremes of society's ills.	Tit. 2:12
Thoroughness	Realizing that each of our tasks will be reviewed and rewarded by God.	Pro. 18:15
Thriftiness	Not letting myself or others spend that which is not necessary.	Luke 16:11
Tolerance	Viewing every person as a valuable individual whom God created and loves.	Phi. 2:2
Truthfulness	Earning future trust by accurately reporting facts.	Eph. 4:25

THE SERVANT PURPOSE

Character Traits	Definition	Bible Verse
Understanding	The ability to reason and comprehend situations.	Psa. 119:34
Wisdom	Seeing and responding to life situations from God's frame of reference.	Pro. 9:10
Virtue	The influence God is having on others through my life regardless of my past failures.	2 Pet. 1:3
Zealous	Maintaining our enthusiasm for our faith and call, not allowing our church or us to fall into a rut of meaningless rhetoric.	Luke 2:49

In this chapter you used your Spiritual Gift to determine you personal vision statement. Your personal vision provides you with your servant focus. As a man seeks a wife, he will be able to determine if the perspective wife can help him. As a woman decides on her choice for a husband, she will have the knowledge to determine if she can help that perspective husband in his God ordained purpose. In the next chapter, you will outline your goals in eight different areas.

**THE
SERVANT
PURPOSE**

6
Servant Goals

Know ye not that they which run in a race run all, but one receiveth the prize? So run, that ye may obtain. And every man that striveth for the mastery is temperate in all things. Now they do it to obtain a corruptible crown; but we an incorruptible. I therefore so run, not as uncertainly; so fight I, not as one that beateth the air: But I keep under my body, and bring it into subjection: lest that by any means, when I have preached to others, I myself should be a castaway (1 Corinthian 9:24-27).

In the previous chapter you developed your personal vision. Now it is time to develop your goals. Goals are important because they provide you with a roadmap of what you desire to accomplish in life. It is important to know your goals before you select someone to marry. You should have a least a few if not many goals in common before you decide to marry.

You will develop goals in the following areas:

- Spiritual
- Family
- Social
- Education
- Physical
- Employment/Work
- Recreation/Fun
- Financial

SERVANT GOALS

First we will begin with spiritual goals. Spiritual goals are the most important goals in a marriage. As a single person, you should outline your spiritual goals as well as why they are important to you. The lack of spiritual goals is one of the primary reasons why so many married couples have challenges in their marriages. Without spiritual goals, married couples will have difficulty accomplishing the purposes for which God brought them together as one.

List your top ten spiritual goals:

1. _____
2. _____
3. _____
4. _____
5. _____
6. _____
7. _____
8. _____
9. _____
10. _____

SERVANT GOALS

Next you will explain why each spiritual goal is important. This will enable you to reflect on your spiritual desires before you get married. In that way you are better informed as you continue the selection process before marriage.

Spiritual goal 1: _____

_____

_____

_____

_____

_____

_____

Spiritual goal 2: _____

_____

_____

_____

_____

_____

_____

SERVANT GOALS

Spiritual goal 3: _____
_____
_____
_____
_____
_____
_____

Spiritual goal 4: _____
_____
_____
_____
_____
_____
_____

SERVANT GOALS

Spiritual goal 5: _____

_____

_____

_____

_____

_____

_____

Spiritual goal 6: _____

_____

_____

_____

_____

_____

_____

SERVANT GOALS

Spiritual goal 7: _____

_____

_____

_____

_____

_____

_____

Spiritual goal 8: _____

_____

_____

_____

_____

_____

_____

SERVANT GOALS

Spiritual goal 9: _____
_____
_____
_____
_____
_____
_____

Spiritual goal 10: _____
_____
_____
_____
_____
_____
_____

SERVANT GOALS

Now you will list your top ten family goals. Think about what you desire for your future family.

1. _____
2. _____
3. _____
4. _____
5. _____
6. _____
7. _____
8. _____
9. _____
10. _____

SERVANT GOALS

Explain why each family goal is important.

Family goal 1: _____

_____
_____
_____
_____
_____
_____

Family goal 2: _____

_____
_____
_____
_____
_____
_____

SERVANT GOALS

Family goal 3: _____
_____
_____
_____
_____
_____
_____

Family goal 4: _____
_____
_____
_____
_____
_____
_____

SERVANT GOALS

Family goal 5: _____

_____

_____

_____

_____

_____

_____

Family goal 6: _____

_____

_____

_____

_____

_____

_____

SERVANT GOALS

Family goal 7: _____
_____
_____
_____
_____
_____
_____

Family goal 8: _____
_____
_____
_____
_____
_____
_____

SERVANT GOALS

Family goal 9: _____

_____

_____

_____

_____

_____

_____

Family goal 10: _____

_____

_____

_____

_____

_____

_____

SERVANT GOALS

List your top ten education goals.

1. _____
2. _____
3. _____
4. _____
5. _____
6. _____
7. _____
8. _____
9. _____
10. _____

SERVANT GOALS

Explain why each education goal is important.

Education goal 1: _____

_____
_____
_____
_____
_____
_____
_____

Education goal 2: _____

_____
_____
_____
_____
_____
_____
_____

SERVANT GOALS

Education goal 3: _____

_____

_____

_____

_____

_____

_____

Education goal 4: _____

_____

_____

_____

_____

_____

_____

SERVANT GOALS

Education goal 5: _____

_____

_____

_____

_____

_____

_____

Education goal 6: _____

_____

_____

_____

_____

_____

_____

SERVANT
GOALS

Education goal 7: _____

_____

_____

_____

_____

_____

_____

Education goal 8: _____

_____

_____

_____

_____

_____

_____

SERVANT GOALS

Education goal 9: _____

_____

_____

_____

_____

_____

_____

Education goal 10: _____

_____

_____

_____

_____

_____

_____

SERVANT GOALS

List your top ten physical goals.

1. _____
2. _____
3. _____
4. _____
5. _____
6. _____
7. _____
8. _____
9. _____
10. _____

SERVANT GOALS

Explain why each physical goal is important.

Physical goal 1: _____

_____

_____

_____

_____

_____

_____

Physical goal 2: _____

_____

_____

_____

_____

_____

_____

SERVANT GOALS

Physical goal 3: _____

_____
_____
_____
_____
_____
_____

Physical goal 4: _____

_____
_____
_____
_____
_____
_____

SERVANT GOALS

Physical goal 5: _____

_____

_____

_____

_____

_____

_____

Physical goal 6: _____

_____

_____

_____

_____

_____

_____

SERVANT
GOALS

Physical goal 7: _____

_____

_____

_____

_____

_____

_____

Physical goal 8: _____

_____

_____

_____

_____

_____

_____

SERVANT GOALS

Physical goal 9: _____

_____

_____

_____

_____

_____

_____

Physical goal 10: _____

_____

_____

_____

_____

_____

_____

SERVANT GOALS

List your top ten employment/work goals.

1. _____
2. _____
3. _____
4. _____
5. _____
6. _____
7. _____
8. _____
9. _____
10. _____

SERVANT GOALS

Explain why each employment/work goal is important.

Employment/Work goal 1: _____

_____
_____
_____
_____
_____
_____

Employment/Work goal 2: _____

_____
_____
_____
_____
_____
_____

SERVANT GOALS

Employment/Work goal 3: _____
_____
_____
_____
_____
_____
_____

Employment/Work goal 4: _____
_____
_____
_____
_____
_____
_____

SERVANT GOALS

Employment/Work goal 5: _____

_____

_____

_____

_____

_____

_____

Employment/Work goal 6: _____

_____

_____

_____

_____

_____

_____

SERVANT
GOALS

Employment/Work goal 7: _____

_____

_____

_____

_____

_____

_____

Employment/Work goal 8: _____

_____

_____

_____

_____

_____

_____

SERVANT GOALS

Employment/Work goal 9: _____

_____

_____

_____

_____

_____

_____

Employment/Work goal 10: _____

_____

_____

_____

_____

_____

_____

SERVANT GOALS

List your top ten recreation/fun goals.

1. _____
2. _____
3. _____
4. _____
5. _____
6. _____
7. _____
8. _____
9. _____
10. _____

SERVANT GOALS

Explain why each recreation/fun goal is important.

Recreation/Fun goal 1: _____

_____

_____

_____

_____

_____

_____

Recreation/Fun goal 2: _____

_____

_____

_____

_____

_____

_____

SERVANT GOALS

Recreation/Fun goal 3: _____
_____
_____
_____
_____
_____
_____

Recreation/Fun goal 4: _____
_____
_____
_____
_____
_____
_____

SERVANT GOALS

Recreation/Fun goal 5: _____
_____
_____
_____
_____
_____
_____
_____

Recreation/Fun goal 6: _____
_____
_____
_____
_____
_____
_____
_____

SERVANT
GOALS

Recreation/Fun goal 7: _____
_____
_____
_____
_____
_____
_____

Recreation/Fun goal 8: _____
_____
_____
_____
_____
_____
_____

SERVANT GOALS

Recreation/Fun goal 9: _____

_____

_____

_____

_____

_____

_____

Recreation/Fun goal 10: _____

_____

_____

_____

_____

_____

_____

SERVANT GOALS

List your top ten financial goals.

1. _____
2. _____
3. _____
4. _____
5. _____
6. _____
7. _____
8. _____
9. _____
10. _____

SERVANT GOALS

Explain why each of your financial goals is important.

Financial goal 1: _____

_____

_____

_____

_____

_____

_____

Financial goal 2: _____

_____

_____

_____

_____

_____

_____

SERVANT GOALS

Financial goal 3: _____
_____
_____
_____
_____
_____
_____

Financial goal 4: _____
_____
_____
_____
_____
_____
_____

SERVANT GOALS

Financial goal 5: _____

_____

_____

_____

_____

_____

_____

Financial goal 6: _____

_____

_____

_____

_____

_____

_____

SERVANT GOALS

Financial goal 7: _____
_____
_____
_____
_____
_____
_____

Financial goal 8: _____
_____
_____
_____
_____
_____
_____

SERVANT GOALS

Financial goal 9: _____

_____

_____

_____

_____

_____

_____

Financial goal 10: _____

_____

_____

_____

_____

_____

_____

You have completed you goals in eight different areas. You have determined why each goal is important to you. As a man decides on who to marry, it is important that he and his perspective wife have some goals in common. This is the same for the woman who decides to marry a perspective husband. Knowing and

SERVANT GOALS

understanding each others goals will enhance the unity in your future marriage and therefore decrease the probability of divorce.

One of the greatest challenges that Adam and Eve had in the Garden of Eden was obeying God's instructions. This could become a challenge for your future marriage too. In the next chapter, you will study several of God's commands and practice following those commands. Then once you get married and God gives you commands it becomes easier to follow those commands and receive the benefits and blessings associated with trusting God.

7

Commands from God

"If ye love me, keep my commandments" (John 14:15).

One of the greatest challenges that the husband and wife will face in the marriage is their willingness to follows God's commands. After God provided Adam with his purpose to serve and the resources, he provided Adam with two specific commands

And the LORD God commanded the man, saying, Of every tree of the garden thou mayest freely eat: But of the tree of the knowledge of good and evil, thou shalt not eat of it: for in the day that thou eatest thereof thou shalt surely die (Genesis 2:16-17).

God told Adam what he could do and what he could not do. Adam and Eve had challenges following God's commands which is evidenced by their eventual departure from the Garden of Eden. The man and woman who decide to marry must remember that there are benefits and blessings to obeying God's commands.

Abraham provides an example of a man who made a concentrated effort to obey God. Till the age of seventy, Abram sojourned among his family in his native country of Chaldea. He then, with his father, his family and household, moved to

COMMANDS FROM GOD

the city of Ur, where he remained for fifteen years. The cause of his movement was a call from God (Acts 7:2-4).

Abram received a second call, accompanied by a promise from God (Gen. 12:1, 2). He trusted God to be the guide for him. Passing along the valley of the Jabbok, in the land of Canaan, he formed his first encampment at Sichem (Gen. 12:6). There he received the great promise, "I will make of thee a great nation," etc. (Gen. 12:2, 3, 7). His entire family then moved northward, and returned to their previous station near Bethel.

After returning to Canaan a dispute arose between Lot's shepherds and those of Abram about water and pasturage. Abram generously gave Lot his choice of the pasture-ground. Lot chose the well-watered plain in which Sodom was situated and thus Abraham whose was Lot's uncle were separated.

Sarai, who was seventy-five years old, became impatient with the promise and persuaded Abram to take Hagar, her Egyptian maid. Ishmael was born and brought up as the heir of the promises in Genesis chapter 16.

God changed Abrahams name to Abram (Genesis. 17:4, 5), and the rite of circumcision was instituted as a sign of the covenant. It was then announced that the heir to these covenant promises would be the son of Sarai. Even though she was now ninety years old, God directed that his name should be Isaac.

At the same time, in commemoration of the promises, Sarai's name was changed to Sarah. Jealousy arose between Sarah and Hagar, whose son, Ishmael, was no longer to be regarded as Abraham's heir. Even though Abram did not agree, Sarah insisted that both Hagar and her son should be sent away.

The next time we see his faith put to the test by a command from God is when He told Abram to go and offer up Isaac who was the heir of all the promises. Abram obeyed God and proceeded in unhesitating obedience to carry out the command. When he was about to slay his Isaac, his uplifted hand was stopped by the angel of God. A ram, which was entangled in a nearby bush, was provided as the offering instead of Isaac.

COMMANDS FROM GOD

Along with Adam and Eve Saul provides the disadvantage for disobeying God. The Amalekites were one of the tribes dwelling in the southern part of Canaan. When the Israelites left Egypt and set out toward Canaan (Exodus 17:8), they were one of the first nations the Israelites encountered.

"Remember what Amalek did to you along the way when you came out from Egypt, how he met you along the way and attacked among you all the stragglers at your rear when you were faint and weary; and he did not fear God". Therefore it shall come about when the LORD your God has given you rest from all your surrounding enemies, in the land which the LORD your God gives you as an inheritance to possess, you shall blot out the memory of Amalek from under heaven; you must not forget (Deuteronomy 25:17-19).

Saul's disobedience is committed by his partial obedience. Saul sins by failing to obey God's commandment to the letter. Saul said he and the people spared the best of the flocks to sacrifice to the Lord.

Now, they may have intended to do this, but their motivation is probably self-serving. The slaughter of all the cattle, as God had commanded, would be a sacrifice too, but the people will not be able to eat any of it. Sparing the animals as they did and then sacrificing them to God accomplished at least two things. First, the people got a free meal at God's expense. They were able to share in the sacrificial meal. And second, they were able to sacrifice the cattle to God in place of their own, thus avoiding any real sacrifice on their part. The point is that Saul's disobedience has a religious perspective, but at its core, it is a self-serving sin. Thus, Saul's actions are hypocritical, appearing to be religious when they are actually pagan.

Saul did not act alone. When he first speaks to Samuel, he is willing to talk of his self-defined obedience in first person terms: "I have performed the command of the LORD" (1 Samuel 15:13). But once it is apparent that his "obedience" is unacceptable to God, Saul suddenly seeks to place the blame on the people of Israel. Only after his excuses were rejected and his sin exposed by Samuel does Saul admit to his role in this sin, along with the people.

COMMANDS FROM GOD

Then Saul said to Samuel, "I have sinned; I have indeed transgressed the command of the LORD and your words, because I feared the people and listened to their voice" (1 Samuel 15:24).

The ending result to Saul's disobedience is that God eventually removed Saul as king.

God has provided twelve commandments that are beneficial for men and women to embrace. Table 2 reveals the twelve commandments which form the foundation for the values that all of God's people should follow.

Table 2

Commandment		Scripture
1.	*No other gods*	Exodus 20:3 (KJV)
2.	*No idols*	Exodus 20:4-6 (KJV)
3.	*Do not take name in vain*	Exodus 20:7 (KJV)
4.	*Keep Sabbath holy*	Exodus 20:8-11 (KJV)
5.	*Honor father and mother*	Exodus 20:12 (KJV)
6.	*Do not murder*	Exodus 20:13 (KJV)
7.	*Do not commit adultery*	Exodus 20:14 (KJV)
8.	*Do not steal*	Exodus 20:15 (KJV)
9.	*Do not give false testimony*	Exodus 20:16 (KJV)
10.	*Do not covet*	Exodus 20:17 (KJV)
11.	*Love the Lord thy God with all thy heart, soul, and mind*	Matthew 22:37 (KJV)
12.	*Love thy neighbour as thyself*	Matthew 22:39 (KJV)

COMMANDS FROM GOD

Complete the following activities to better understand the commandments that God requires you to follow.

Note: Review this section before starting to ensure that you have access to the necessary materials needed to finish.

Commandment 1:   Exodus 20:3 KJV

Book: Exodus   **Chapter:** 20   **Verse:** 3

Write the KJV verse here: _____

_____

_____

_____

_____

What are the three key words for this verse?

1. _____

2. _____

3. _____

Compare the KJV verse with the Amplified version:

_____

_____

_____

ADVANCED MARRIAGE TRAINING FOR SINGLES

COMMANDS FROM GOD

Compare the KJV verse with the New American Standard version:

_____

_____

_____

_____

Compare the KJV verse with the New International version:

_____

_____

_____

_____

What are the main differences between the versions?

_____

_____

_____

_____

COMMANDS FROM GOD

Are the any scriptures that are similar to the verse?

_____

_____

_____

_____

Now that you have completed the verse study for the first commandment you will complete the word study for this first commandment.

Write the first key word here: _____

Greek or Hebrew form: _____

What other scriptures have the same form for this word?

_____

_____

_____

What is the Strong's number? _____

ADVANCED MARRIAGE TRAINING FOR SINGLES

COMMANDS FROM GOD

What is the definition from the Strong's concordance?

_____
_____
_____
_____

What is the importance of this word in the verse?

_____
_____
_____
_____

What is your opinion regarding the word you have studied?

_____
_____
_____
_____
_____

COMMANDS FROM GOD

Write the second key word here: _____

Greek or Hebrew form: _____

What other scriptures have the same form for this word?

_____

_____

_____

What is the Strong's number: _____

What is the definition from the Strong's concordance?

_____

_____

_____

_____

_____

COMMANDS FROM GOD

What is the importance of this word in the verse?

_____
_____
_____
_____

What is your opinion regarding the word you have studied?

_____
_____
_____
_____

Write the third key word here: _____

Greek or Hebrew form: _____

COMMANDS FROM GOD

What other scriptures have the same form for this word?

_____

_____

_____

What is the Strong's number? _____

What is the definition from the Strong's concordance?

_____

_____

_____

_____

_____

What is the importance of this word in the verse?

_____

_____

_____

_____

_____

_____

COMMANDS FROM GOD

What is your opinion regarding the word you have studied?

_____

_____

_____

_____

COMMANDS FROM GOD

Commandment 2: Exodus 20:4-6 KJV

Book: Exodus **Chapter:** 20 **Verse:** 4-6

Write the KJV verse here: _____

_____

_____

_____

_____

What are the three key words for this verse?

1. _____

2. _____

3. _____

Compare the KJV verse with the Amplified version:

_____

_____

_____

_____

_____

COMMANDS FROM GOD

Compare the KJV verse with the New American Standard version:

_____

_____

_____

_____

Compare the KJV verse with the New International version:

_____

_____

_____

_____

What are the main differences between the versions?

_____

_____

_____

_____

COMMANDS FROM GOD

Are the any scriptures that are similar to the verse?

_____

_____

_____

_____

Now that you have completed the verse study for the second commandment you will complete the word study for this second commandment.

Write the first key word here: _____

Greek or Hebrew form: _____

What other scriptures have the same form for this word?

_____

_____

_____

What is the Strong's number? _____

COMMANDS FROM GOD

What is the definition from the Strong's concordance?

_____
_____
_____
_____

What is the importance of this word in the verse?

_____
_____
_____
_____

What is your opinion regarding the word you have studied?

_____
_____
_____
_____
_____

COMMANDS FROM GOD

Write the second key word here: _____

Greek or Hebrew form: _____

What other scriptures have the same form for this word?

_____

_____

_____

What is the Strong's number: _____

What is the definition from the Strong's concordance?

_____

_____

_____

_____

_____

COMMANDS FROM GOD

What is the importance of this word in the verse?

_____
_____
_____
_____
_____

What is your opinion regarding the word you have studied?

_____
_____
_____
_____
_____

Write the third key word here: _____

Greek or Hebrew form: _____

COMMANDS FROM GOD

What other scriptures have the same form for this word?

_____

_____

_____

What is the Strong's number? _____

What is the definition from the Strong's concordance?

_____

_____

_____

_____

_____

What is the importance of this word in the verse?

_____

_____

_____

_____

_____

COMMANDS FROM GOD

What is your opinion regarding the word you have studied?

_____

_____

_____

_____

_____

COMMANDS FROM GOD

Commandment 3: Exodus 20:7 KJV

Book: Exodus **Chapter:** 20 **Verse:** 7

Write the KJV verse here: _____

_____

_____

_____

_____

What are the three key words for this verse?

1. _____

2. _____

3. _____

Compare the KJV verse with the Amplified version:

_____

_____

_____

_____

COMMANDS FROM GOD

Compare the KJV verse with the New American Standard version:

_____
_____
_____
_____

Compare the KJV verse with the New International version:

_____
_____
_____
_____

What are the main differences between the versions?

_____
_____
_____
_____

COMMANDS FROM GOD

Are the any scriptures that are similar to the verse?

_____

_____

_____

_____

Now that you have completed the verse study for the commandment you will complete the word study for this third commandment.

Write the first key word here: _____

Greek or Hebrew form: _____

What other scriptures have the same form for this word?

_____

_____

_____

What is the Strong's number? _____

ADVANCED MARRIAGE TRAINING FOR SINGLES

COMMANDS FROM GOD

What is the definition from the Strong's concordance?

_____
_____
_____
_____

What is the importance of this word in the verse?

_____
_____
_____
_____

What is your opinion regarding the word you have studied?

_____
_____
_____
_____

COMMANDS FROM GOD

Write the second key word here: _____

Greek or Hebrew form: _____

What other scriptures have the same form for this word?

_____

_____

_____

What is the Strong's number: _____

What is the definition from the Strong's concordance?

_____

_____

_____

_____

_____

COMMANDS FROM GOD

What is the importance of this word in the verse?

_____
_____
_____
_____

What is your opinion regarding the word you have studied?

_____
_____
_____
_____
_____

Write the third key word here: _____

Greek or Hebrew form: _____

COMMANDS FROM GOD

What other scriptures have the same form for this word?

_____
_____
_____

What is the Strong's number? _____

What is the definition from the Strong's concordance?

_____
_____
_____
_____
_____

What is the importance of this word in the verse?

_____
_____
_____
_____
_____

COMMANDS FROM GOD

What is your opinion regarding the word you have studied?

_____

_____

_____

_____

_____

COMMANDS FROM GOD

Commandment 4:   Exodus 20:8-11 KJV

Book: Exodus   **Chapter:** 20   **Verse:** 8-11

Write the KJV verse here: _____

_____

_____

_____

_____

What are the three key words for this verse?

1. _____

2. _____

3. _____

Compare the KJV verse with the Amplified version:

_____

_____

_____

_____

_____

COMMANDS FROM GOD

Compare the KJV verse with the New American Standard version:

_____

_____

_____

_____

Compare the KJV verse with the New International version:

_____

_____

_____

_____

What are the main differences between the versions?

_____

_____

_____

_____

COMMANDS FROM GOD

Are the any scriptures that are similar to the verse?

_____

_____

_____

_____

Now that you have completed the verse study for the fourth commandment you will complete the word study for this fourth commandment.

Write the first key word here: _____

Greek or Hebrew form: _____

What other scriptures have the same form for this word?

_____

_____

_____

What is the Strong's number? _____

COMMANDS FROM GOD

What is the definition from the Strong's concordance?

_____
_____
_____
_____

What is the importance of this word in the verse?

_____
_____
_____
_____

What is your opinion regarding the word you have studied?

_____
_____
_____
_____

COMMANDS FROM GOD

Write the second key word here: _____

Greek or Hebrew form: _____

What other scriptures have the same form for this word?

_____
_____
_____

What is the Strong's number: _____

What is the definition from the Strong's concordance?

_____
_____
_____
_____
_____

COMMANDS FROM GOD

What is the importance of this word in the verse?

_____
_____
_____
_____
_____

What is your opinion regarding the word you have studied?

_____
_____
_____
_____
_____

Write the third key word here: _____

Greek or Hebrew form: _____

COMMANDS FROM GOD

What other scriptures have the same form for this word?
_____
_____
_____

What is the Strong's number? _____

What is the definition from the Strong's concordance?
_____
_____
_____
_____
_____

What is the importance of this word in the verse?
_____
_____
_____
_____
_____

COMMANDS FROM GOD

What is your opinion regarding the word you have studied?

_____

_____

_____

_____

_____

COMMANDS FROM GOD

Commandment 5: Exodus 20:12 KJV

Book: Exodus **Chapter:** 20 **Verse:** 12

Write the KJV verse here: _____

_____

_____

_____

_____

What are the three key words for this verse?

1. _____

2. _____

3. _____

Compare the KJV verse with the Amplified version:

_____

_____

_____

_____

COMMANDS FROM GOD

Compare the KJV verse with the New American Standard version:

_____
_____
_____
_____

Compare the KJV verse with the New International version:

_____
_____
_____
_____

What are the main differences between the versions?

_____
_____
_____
_____

COMMANDS FROM GOD

Are the any scriptures that are similar to the verse?

_____

_____

_____

_____

Now that you have completed the verse study for the commandment you will complete the word study for this fifth commandment.

Write the first key word here: _____

Greek or Hebrew form: _____

What other scriptures have the same form for this word?

_____

_____

_____

What is the Strong's number? _____

COMMANDS FROM GOD

What is the definition from the Strong's concordance?

_____
_____
_____
_____

What is the importance of this word in the verse?

_____
_____
_____
_____

What is your opinion regarding the word you have studied?

_____
_____
_____
_____
_____

COMMANDS FROM GOD

Write the second key word here: _____

Greek or Hebrew form: _____

What other scriptures have the same form for this word?

_____
_____
_____

What is the Strong's number: _____

What is the definition from the Strong's concordance?

_____
_____
_____
_____
_____

COMMANDS FROM GOD

What is the importance of this word in the verse?

_____
_____
_____
_____
_____

What is your opinion regarding the word you have studied?

_____
_____
_____
_____
_____

Write the third key word here: _____

Greek or Hebrew form: _____

COMMANDS FROM GOD

What other scriptures have the same form for this word?
_____
_____
_____

What is the Strong's number? _____

What is the definition from the Strong's concordance?
_____
_____
_____
_____
_____

What is the importance of this word in the verse?
_____
_____
_____
_____
_____

COMMANDS FROM GOD

What is your opinion regarding the word you have studied?

_____

_____

_____

_____

_____

COMMANDS FROM GOD

Commandment 6: Exodus 20:12 KJV

Book: Exodus   **Chapter:** 20   **Verse:** 12

Write the KJV verse here: _____

_____

_____

_____

_____

What are the three key words for this verse?

1. _____

2. _____

3. _____

Compare the KJV verse with the Amplified version:

_____

_____

_____

_____

ADVANCED MARRIAGE TRAINING FOR SINGLES

COMMANDS FROM GOD

Compare the KJV verse with the New American Standard version:

_____
_____
_____
_____

Compare the KJV verse with the New International version:

_____
_____
_____
_____

What are the main differences between the versions?

_____
_____
_____
_____

COMMANDS FROM GOD

Are the any scriptures that are similar to the verse?

_____
_____
_____
_____
_____

Now that you have completed the verse study for the commandment you will complete the word study for this sixth commandment.

Write the first key word here: _____

Greek or Hebrew form: _____

What other scriptures have the same form for this word?

_____
_____
_____

What is the Strong's number? _____

COMMANDS FROM GOD

What is the definition from the Strong's concordance?

_____

_____

_____

_____

What is the importance of this word in the verse?

_____

_____

_____

_____

What is your opinion regarding the word you have studied?

_____

_____

_____

_____

_____

COMMANDS FROM GOD

Write the second key word here: _____

Greek or Hebrew form: _____

What other scriptures have the same form for this word?

_____

_____

_____

What is the Strong's number: _____

What is the definition from the Strong's concordance?

_____

_____

_____

_____

_____

COMMANDS FROM GOD

What is the importance of this word in the verse?

_____
_____
_____
_____
_____

What is your opinion regarding the word you have studied?

_____
_____
_____
_____
_____

Write the third key word here: _____

Greek or Hebrew form: _____

COMMANDS FROM GOD

What other scriptures have the same form for this word?
_____
_____
_____

What is the Strong's number? _____

What is the definition from the Strong's concordance?
_____
_____
_____
_____
_____

What is the importance of this word in the verse?
_____
_____
_____
_____
_____

COMMANDS FROM GOD

What is your opinion regarding the word you have studied?

_____

_____

_____

_____

_____

COMMANDS FROM GOD

Commandment 7: Exodus 20:14 KJV

Book: Exodus **Chapter:** 20 **Verse:** 14

Write the KJV verse here: _____

_____

_____

_____

_____

What are the three key words for this verse?

1. _____

2. _____

3. _____

Compare the KJV verse with the Amplified version:

_____

_____

_____

_____

COMMANDS FROM GOD

Compare the KJV verse with the New American Standard version:

_____
_____
_____
_____

Compare the KJV verse with the New International version:

_____
_____
_____
_____

What are the main differences between the versions?

_____
_____
_____
_____

COMMANDS FROM GOD

Are the any scriptures that are similar to the verse?

_____
_____
_____
_____
_____

Now that you have completed the verse study for the commandment you will complete the word study for this seventh commandment.

Write the first key word here: _____

Greek or Hebrew form: _____

What other scriptures have the same form for this word?

_____
_____
_____

What is the Strong's number? _____

COMMANDS FROM GOD

What is the definition from the Strong's concordance?

_____
_____
_____
_____
_____

What is the importance of this word in the verse?

_____
_____
_____
_____
_____

What is your opinion regarding the word you have studied?

_____
_____
_____
_____
_____
_____

COMMANDS FROM GOD

Write the second key word here: _____

Greek or Hebrew form: _____

What other scriptures have the same form for this word?

_____

_____

_____

What is the Strong's number: _____

What is the definition from the Strong's concordance?

_____

_____

_____

_____

_____

COMMANDS FROM GOD

What is the importance of this word in the verse?

_____
_____
_____
_____
_____

What is your opinion regarding the word you have studied?

_____
_____
_____
_____
_____

Write the third key word here: _____

Greek or Hebrew form: _____

COMMANDS FROM GOD

What other scriptures have the same form for this word?

_____

_____

_____

What is the Strong's number? _____

What is the definition from the Strong's concordance?

_____

_____

_____

_____

What is the importance of this word in the verse?

_____

_____

_____

_____

_____

COMMANDS FROM GOD

What is your opinion regarding the word you have studied?

_____

_____

_____

_____

COMMANDS FROM GOD

Commandment 8:   Exodus 20:15 KJV

Book: Exodus   **Chapter:** 20   **Verse:** 15

Write the KJV verse here: _____

_____

_____

_____

_____

What are the three key words for this verse?

1. _____

2. _____

3. _____

Compare the KJV verse with the Amplified version:

_____

_____

_____

_____

COMMANDS FROM GOD

Compare the KJV verse with the New American Standard version:

_____

_____

_____

_____

Compare the KJV verse with the New International version:

_____

_____

_____

_____

What are the main differences between the versions?

_____

_____

_____

_____

COMMANDS FROM GOD

Are the any scriptures that are similar to the verse?

_____

_____

_____

_____

_____

Now that you have completed the verse study for the commandment you will complete the word study for this eighth commandment.

Write the first key word here: _____

Greek or Hebrew form: _____

What other scriptures have the same form for this word?

_____

_____

_____

ADVANCED MARRIAGE TRAINING FOR SINGLES

COMMANDS FROM GOD

What is the Strong's number? _____

What is the definition from the Strong's concordance?

_____

_____

_____

_____

_____

What is the importance of this word in the verse?

_____

_____

_____

_____

_____

COMMANDS FROM GOD

What is your opinion regarding the word you have studied?

_____
_____
_____
_____
_____

Write the second key word here: _____

Greek or Hebrew form: _____

What other scriptures have the same form for this word?

_____
_____
_____

What is the Strong's number? _____

COMMANDS FROM GOD

What is the definition from the Strong's concordance?

_____

_____

_____

_____

What is the importance of this word in the verse?

_____

_____

_____

_____

What is your opinion regarding the word you have studied?

_____

_____

_____

_____

_____

COMMANDS FROM GOD

Write the third key word here: _____

Greek or Hebrew form: _____

What other scriptures have the same form for this word?

_____

_____

_____

What is the Strong's number: _____

What is the definition from the Strong's concordance?

_____

_____

_____

_____

_____

COMMANDS FROM GOD

What is the importance of this word in the verse?

_____

_____

_____

_____

_____

What is your opinion regarding the word you have studied?

_____

_____

_____

_____

_____

COMMANDS FROM GOD

Commandment 9: Exodus 20:16 KJV

Book: Exodus **Chapter:** 20 **Verse:** 3

Write the KJV verse here: _____

_____
_____
_____
_____

What are the three key words for this verse?

1. _____
2. _____
3. _____

Compare the KJV verse with the Amplified version:

_____
_____
_____
_____

COMMANDS FROM GOD

Compare the KJV verse with the New American Standard version:

_____

_____

_____

_____

Compare the KJV verse with the New International version:

_____

_____

_____

_____

What are the main differences between the versions?

_____

_____

_____

_____

COMMANDS FROM GOD

Are the any scriptures that are similar to the verse?

_____
_____
_____
_____

Now that you have completed the verse study for the commandment you will complete the word study for this ninth commandment.

Write the first key word here: _____

Greek or Hebrew form: _____

What other scriptures have the same form for this word?

_____
_____
_____

What is the Strong's number? _____

COMMANDS FROM GOD

What is the definition from the Strong's concordance?

_____
_____
_____
_____
_____

What is the importance of this word in the verse?

_____
_____
_____
_____
_____

What is your opinion regarding the word you have studied?

_____
_____
_____
_____
_____

COMMANDS FROM GOD

Write the second
key word here: _____

Greek or Hebrew
form: _____

What other scriptures have the same form for this word?

_____

_____

_____

What is the Strong's
number?   _____

What is the definition from the Strong's concordance?

_____

_____

_____

_____

_____

COMMANDS FROM GOD

What is the importance of this word in the verse?

_____
_____
_____
_____

What is your opinion regarding the word you have studied?

_____
_____
_____
_____

Write the third key word here: _____

Greek or Hebrew form: _____

COMMANDS FROM GOD

What other scriptures have the same form for this word?

_____
_____
_____

What is the Strong's number? _____

What is the definition from the Strong's concordance?

_____
_____
_____
_____
_____

What is the importance of this word in the verse?

_____
_____
_____
_____
_____

COMMANDS FROM GOD

What is your opinion regarding the word you have studied?

_____

_____

_____

_____

_____

COMMANDS FROM GOD

Commandment 10: Exodus 20:17 KJV

Book: Exodus **Chapter:** 20 **Verse:** 17

Write the KJV verse here: _____

_____

_____

_____

_____

What are the three key words for this verse?

1._____

2._____

3._____

Compare the KJV verse with the Amplified version:

_____

_____

_____

_____

COMMANDS FROM GOD

Compare the KJV verse with the New American Standard version:

_____
_____
_____
_____

Compare the KJV verse with the New International version:

_____
_____
_____
_____

What are the main differences between the versions?

_____
_____
_____
_____

COMMANDS FROM GOD

Are the any scriptures that are similar to the verse?

_____
_____
_____
_____
_____

Now that you have completed the verse study for the commandment you will complete the word study for this tenth commandment.

Write the first key word here: _____

Greek or Hebrew form: _____

What other scriptures have the same form for this word?

_____
_____
_____

What is the Strong's number? _____

COMMANDS FROM GOD

What is the definition from the Strong's concordance?

_____
_____
_____
_____

What is the importance of this word in the verse?

_____
_____
_____
_____

What is your opinion regarding the word you have studied?

_____
_____
_____
_____

COMMANDS FROM GOD

Write the second
key word here: _____

Greek or Hebrew
form: _____

What other scriptures have the same form for this word?

_____

_____

_____

What is the Strong's
number?   _____

What is the definition from the Strong's concordance?

_____

_____

_____

_____

_____

COMMANDS FROM GOD

What is the importance of this word in the verse?

_____
_____
_____
_____
_____

What is your opinion regarding the word you have studied?

_____
_____
_____
_____
_____

Write the third key word here: _____

Greek or Hebrew form: _____

COMMANDS FROM GOD

What other scriptures have the same form for this word?

_____

_____

_____

What is the Strong's number? _____

What is the definition from the Strong's concordance?

_____

_____

_____

_____

_____

What is the importance of this word in the verse?

_____

_____

_____

_____

_____

_____

COMMANDS FROM GOD

What is your opinion regarding the word you have studied?

_____

_____

_____

_____

COMMANDS FROM GOD

Commandment 11: Matthew 22:37 KJV

Book: Matthew **Chapter:** 22 **Verse:** 37

Write the KJV verse here: _____

_____

_____

_____

_____

What are the three key words for this verse?

1._____

2._____

3._____

Compare the KJV verse with the Amplified version:

_____

_____

_____

_____

COMMANDS FROM GOD

Compare the KJV verse with the New American Standard version:

_____
_____
_____
_____

Compare the KJV verse with the New International version:

_____
_____
_____
_____

What are the main differences between the versions?

_____
_____
_____
_____

COMMANDS FROM GOD

Are the any scriptures that are similar to the verse?

_____

_____

_____

_____

_____

Now that you have completed the verse study for the commandment you will complete the word study for this eleventh commandment.

Write the first key word here: _____

Greek or Hebrew form: _____

What other scriptures have the same form for this word?

_____

_____

_____

What is the Strong's number? _____

ADVANCED MARRIAGE TRAINING FOR SINGLES

COMMANDS FROM GOD

What is the definition from the Strong's concordance?

_____

_____

_____

_____

_____

What is the importance of this word in the verse?

_____

_____

_____

_____

_____

COMMANDS FROM GOD

What is your opinion regarding the word you have studied?

_____

_____

_____

_____

_____

Write the second key word here: _____

Greek or Hebrew form: _____

What other scriptures have the same form for this word?

_____

_____

_____

What is the Strong's number? _____

COMMANDS FROM GOD

What is the definition from the Strong's concordance?

_____
_____
_____
_____

What is the importance of this word in the verse?

_____
_____
_____
_____

What is your opinion regarding the word you have studied?

_____
_____
_____
_____
_____

COMMANDS FROM GOD

Write the third key word here: _____

Greek or Hebrew form: _____

What other scriptures have the same form for this word?

_____

_____

_____

What is the Strong's number: _____

What is the definition from the Strong's concordance?

_____

_____

_____

_____

_____

COMMANDS FROM GOD

What is the importance of this word in the verse?

_____
_____
_____
_____
_____

What is your opinion regarding the word you have studied?

_____
_____
_____
_____
_____
_____

COMMANDS FROM GOD

Commandment 12:   Matthew 22:39 KJV

Book: Matthew   **Chapter:** 22   **Verse:** 39

Write the KJV verse here: _____

_____

_____

_____

_____

What are the three key words for this verse?

1. _____

2. _____

3. _____

Compare the KJV verse with the Amplified version:

_____

_____

_____

_____

COMMANDS FROM GOD

Compare the KJV verse with the New American Standard version:

_____

_____

_____

_____

Compare the KJV verse with the New International version:

_____

_____

_____

_____

What are the main differences between the versions?

_____

_____

_____

_____

COMMANDS FROM GOD

Are the any scriptures that are similar to the verse?

_____
_____
_____
_____
_____

Now that you have completed the verse study for the commandment you will complete the word study for this twelfth commandment.

Write the first key word here: _____

Greek or Hebrew form: _____

What other scriptures have the same form for this word?

_____
_____
_____

What is the Strong's number? _____

COMMANDS FROM GOD

What is the definition from the Strong's concordance?

_____
_____
_____
_____
_____

What is the importance of this word in the verse?

_____
_____
_____
_____
_____

What is your opinion regarding the word you have studied?

_____
_____
_____
_____
_____

COMMANDS FROM GOD

Write the second
key word here: _____

Greek or Hebrew
form: _____

What other scriptures have the same form for this word?

_____

_____

_____

What is the Strong's
number: _____

What is the definition from the Strong's concordance?

_____

_____

_____

_____

_____

COMMANDS FROM GOD

What is the importance of this word in the verse?

_____
_____
_____
_____
_____

What is your opinion regarding the word you have studied?

_____
_____
_____
_____
_____

Write the third key word here: _____

Greek or Hebrew form: _____

COMMANDS FROM GOD

What other scriptures have the same form for this word?

_____
_____
_____

What is the Strong's number? _____

What is the definition from the Strong's concordance?

_____
_____
_____
_____
_____

What is the importance of this word in the verse?

_____
_____
_____
_____
_____

COMMANDS FROM GOD

What is your opinion regarding the word you have studied?

_____
_____
_____
_____
_____

You have successfully completed a study of God's ten commandments. Adam and Eve were tripped up because they did not obey God's commandments. They were kicked out of the Garden of Eden because of their disobedience. As a single person you have an opportunity to put into practice obeying God's commands. This will provide the foundation for future obedience behavior after you are married.

After you get married, there are going to be instances where the husband and wife do not agree. If there are not mechanisms in place that reduce tension in the marriage, then the communication between the husband and wife can become explosive and therefore lead to separation or divorce. In the next chapter you will learn to use an instrument designed to reduce conflict in the marriage.

8
Conflict Reflection

Moreover if thy brother shall trespass against thee, go and tell him his fault between thee and him alone: if he shall hear thee, thou hast gained thy brother. But if he will not hear [thee, then] take with thee one or two more, that in the mouth of two or three witnesses every word may be established. And if he shall neglect to hear them, tell [it] unto the church: but if he neglect to hear the church, let him be unto thee as an heathen man and a publican (Matthew 18:15-17).

Conflict management is essential for a successful marriage. According to God's original design, a successful marriage includes three major components. The first component, the husband must be a servant and a godly steward over the resources that God provides. The second component is that the husband and wife must obey God's commands. The third component is that the husband and wife work together as a team in the area of service that God appoints to the husband.

Teamwork is an essential component for success in the marriage. The bible provides two great examples of teamwork. In the Old Testament, Nehemiah called the people of Israel together and convinced them that they could successfully rebuild the wall as a team *(Nehemiah 2:17-18)*. In the New Testament, Jesus sent His disciples out two by two, which afforded them an opportunity to work as a team *(Luke 10:1)*. Teamwork between the husband and wife provides opportunities for encouragement in times of rejection. However, during the difficult times the communication between the husband and wife can present challenges for the marriage.

CONFLICT RESOLUTION

Many marriages can become dysfunctional when communication challenges become prominent. Communication problems can result from the defensive mechanisms that were learn as children. As outlined in chapter 2, defensive mechanisms are the unwritten rules an individual learns and utilizes to effectively deal with circumstances that are upsetting, embarrassing, or threatening. When confronted about our defensive routines, we can enter the phase of organizational malaise. Organizational malaise is the final level of a dysfunctional organization. During this phase, the husband and wife will seek to find fault within the marriage rather than accept responsibility for their actions and correct their behavior accordingly. The husband or wife continues the process by accentuating the negative and deemphasizing the positive in an effort to cover up their actions. This phase is further exacerbated by a refusal to discuss their area of responsibility.

As a husband and wife, it is your responsibility to implement strategies that enhance communication in the marriage. Argyris and Schon (1974) developed a left-hand column activity that enables individuals to redevelop and improve their behavior that results from defense mechanisms. For our purposes, I am calling the left-hand column activity the Conflict Reflection Activity. Before we give the details of using this tool, we need to establish some groundwork. We will establish this groundwork through the following example.

Our example includes Tom and Julie. Tom and Julie developed defensive routines that had an adverse impact on their marriage. When Julie was a child, the adults constantly told that her ideas were foolish. To protect herself, she developed a defensive routine that resulted in her agreeing with the adult and then later changing her mind about her decision. Tom faced some of the same challenges. When Tom was a child, he was harassed over anything that he cared about. If he cared about the fish, he was harassed. If he cared about the dog, he was harassed. Anything he cared about, he was harassed. To protect himself, Tom developed a defensive routine. He would not get excited about anything. In that way, it reduced and minimized the harassment.

CONFLICT RESOLUTION

Now, let us fast forward. Tom and Julie are now married and discussing taking a vacation trip to Hawaii. The following is their dialogue.

Julie: Let us vacation in Hawaii this year.

Tom: I do not know if we should do that.

Julie: Why?

Tom: Do you think we should keep the money in the bank and vacation where it is less expensive? Like a local beach.

Julie: We have been saving for this trip for three years. We can cut back on some of the extras and still have some money left in the bank.

Tom: OK

Julie: Tom you might be right!

Tom: Make-up you mind!

Julie: Well you do not seem to be enthusiastic about going to Hawaii anyway!

Tom: Why do you always change your mind!

Julie: Leave me alone! I do not want to talk about it anymore!

As you have read this conversation did not turn out to well. In fact, it ended in a heated argument and both parties shut down the communication channel. The defensive routines of both contributed to the result. Tom responded in anger to Julie when she said, "Tom you might be right!". Remember that Julie's defensive routine was to agree with the person and then change her decision. Julie also

CONFLICT RESOLUTION

responded to Tom by stating, "Well you do not seem to be enthusiastic about going to Hawaii anyway!". Remember that Tom's defensive routine was to protect himself by not getting excited about anything.

This scenario plays out the same way with many couples. The bigger challenge is how do we reverse this process where every conversation with our spouse has a positive ending. As I mentioned before we can use a modification of the left-hand column activity developed by Argyris and Schon (1974).

Either party could use this conflict reflection activity. We are going to focus on Tom. Tom decided to use the activity and he began by retrieving a blank piece of paper. He drew a line down the middle of the paper. On the right side he wrote down what was said during the conversation. On the left side, he wrote down what he was thinking throughout the entire conversation. The next page reveals Tom's finished outline.

CONFLICT RESOLUTION

What I was thinking	What was said
	Julie: Let us vacation in Hawaii this year.
It does not sound exciting.	Tom: I do not know if we should do that.
I am not really interested	Julie: Why?
Just take my word. for it.	Tom: Do you think we should keep the money in the bank and vacation where it is less expensive? Like a local beach.
I want to spend the money on what I want.	Julie: We have been saving for this trip for three years. We can cut back on some of the extras and still have some money left in the bank.
I might be able to get my way.	Tom: OK
Thank you	Julie: Tom you might be right!
She did it again.	Tom: Make-up you mind!
She is so irritating.	Julie: Well you do not seem to be enthusiastic about going to Hawaii anyway.
That is just the way I am.	Tom: Why do you always change your mind!
It's her fault	Julie: Leave me alone! I do not want to talk about it anymore!
Maybe we shouldn't talk at all.	

The final step is to examine his thinking on the left side to determine at what point he had an opportunity to ensure that the conversation remained positive.

CONFLICT RESOLUTION

Where do you believe that Tom had to opportunity to ensure that the conversation between him and his wife remained positive? And why? Write your answer below.

_____

_____

_____

_____

_____

_____

Now it is your turn. Think about an intense argument that you had with someone. In the table on the next page, first complete the right side by writing down what was said during that conversation. Then on the left-hand side, write down what you were thinking. Finally, circle the point in the conversation where you had an opportunity to ensure that the conversation remained positive. What would you have said differently?

After completing the chart, write down what you would have said differently on the lines below.

_____

_____

_____

_____

CONFLICT RESOLUTION

What I Was Thinking	What Was Said

CONFLICT RESOLUTION

What I Was Thinking	What Was Said

CONFLICT RESOLUTION

Now that you have completed the Conflict Reflection Activity, remember to use this tool after you have had an intense conversation with your spouse. All you need is a few blank sheets of paper. Draw a line down the middle of the paper. At the top on the right hand side write down 'what was said' during the conversation. Then, on the left-side write down 'what you were thinking' during the conversation. Finally, circle the point where you had an opportunity to ensure that the conversation remained positive.

We have discussed the importance of communication in the marriage and provided a tool for individuals to use that will enhance marriage communication. In the next chapter, we will complete another activity that will reduce conflict in the marriage.

CONFLICT RESOLUTION

9

Commitment Analysis

Jesus saith unto them, My meat is to do the will of him that sent me, and to finish his work. Say not ye, There are yet four months, and [then] cometh harvest? behold, I say unto you, Lift up your eyes, and look on the fields; for they are white already to harvest. And he that reapeth receiveth wages, and gathereth fruit unto life eternal: that both he that soweth and he that reapeth may rejoice together. And herein is that saying true, One soweth, and another reapeth. I sent you to reap that whereon ye bestowed no labour: other men laboured, and ye are entered into their labours (John 4:34-38).

As outlined in chapter 1, God intends for the husband and wife to work together as a team. We know this because in Genesis 2:18 God made Eve to be Adams helpmeet. When He made Eve, He also introduced the concept of teamwork.

When God made the wife, He made the ultimate team player. He provided the husband with a team player that is committed to the total outcome of the team. In some cases, the ultimate team player will discuss her desires as complaints. The expression is two-fold. The husband may also express his desires as complaints.

COMMITMENT ANALYSIS

The irony is that both spouses who are expressing their complaints are expressing their commitment too. We complain about what we care about. What we care about what we are committed to. When we care about something deep enough we will complain to our spouse.

The problem with complaints is that to many complaints can destroy the marriage. Or the misinterpretation of a complaint can destroy a marriage. To much complaining will result in a negative atmosphere. Too much complaining causes anxiety in the marriage that will cause undo stress for the spouse and depending on how the other spouse reacts can become detrimental for the marriage. One way to offset the impact of excessive complaining is to evaluate your spouses commitments.

In the table on the next page, we have evaluated the complaints of a spouse. In each case, the wives complaints are actually the same things that the husband desires. Now that the husband knows that the complaint is a positive commitment that enhances the livelihood of both spouses, the husband will have a positive response to the complaint. This will enhance the communication between he husband and wife and will ultimately enhance the overall marriage.

COMMITMENT ANALYSIS

Complaint	Commitment
1. He won't cut the grass or weed the garden.	My wife is committed to having a well landscaped house.
2. He won't help me clean the house.	My wife is committed to a clean house.
3. He does not talk to me.	My wife is committed to communication.
4. He won't help me discipline the kids.	My wife is committed to well behaved children.
5. He doesn't participate in family bible studies.	My wife is committed to the spiritual development of her husband.
6. We do not agree on finances.	My wife is committed to financial security.

Now it is your turn. In the table on the next page write down your top ten complaints. Then determine your commitment for each complaint. Instead of complaining to your perspective spouse, you can tell them that "My commitment is ....". This will reduce future miscommunication in your marriage.

COMMITMENT ANALYSIS

Complaint	Commitment
1.	
2.	
3.	
4.	
5.	
6.	
7.	
8.	
9.	
10.	

You have successfully completed the Advanced Marriage Training for Singles curriculum. What a tremendous accomplishment. In chapter 1 you learned about the dysfunctional marriage. In chapter 2 you learned the specific characteristics associated with a dysfunctional marriage. Then you prepared yourself by completing chapters 3 to 9. Now you are equipped for a positive and productive marriage. In the final chapter, I will provide you with some final thoughts.

10

A Final Note

Ye have said, It [is] vain to serve God: and what profit [is it] that we have kept his ordinance, and that we have walked mournfully before the LORD of hosts? And now we call the proud happy; yea, they that work wickedness are set up; yea, [they that] tempt God are even delivered. Then they that feared the LORD spake often one to another: and the LORD hearkened, and heard [it], and a book of remembrance was written before him for them that feared the LORD, and that thought upon his name. And they shall be mine, saith the LORD of hosts, in that day when I make up my jewels; and I will spare them, as a man spareth his own son that serveth him. Then shall ye return, and discern between the righteous and the wicked, between him that serveth God and him that serveth him not (Malachi 3:14-18).

Marriage is the first organization instituted by God. God has a desire for the husband and the wife to have a marriage that glorifies His name. He wants a marriage that impacts the world and makes a difference in the lives of many.

Now that you have completed the Advanced Marriage Training for Singles you are better informed of who is the correct person for you to marry. For future husbands, you will know your area of service and will find a wife that can help you with your calling. For future wives, you know more about yourself and will be able to go into a marriage knowing how to help your perspective husband.

A FINAL NOTE

Since you have completed the God's Commands chapter and put it into practice you are less likely to disobey God's commands once married. This will enhance your marriage because you are willing to trust God with every minute of your marriage.

When the world presents your marriage with the ongoing challenges, the husband and wife will stand tall against all threats because you understand and accept each other goals which will enable the marriage to remain in unity.

When you have communication breakdowns, you now have two tools that will enhance the communication in your marriage. Because you have completed this book you are better prepared and equipped to overcome any challenges that will surface in your marriage. You will not become a divorce statistic like many others because you took the time to understand the original design for marriage and applied the principles before and during the selection process.

References

Argyris, C. (1990). Overcoming Organizational Defenses: Facilitating Organizational Learning. Upper Saddle River, New Jersey: Prentice Hall

Argyris, C., & Schon, D. (1974). *Theory in Practice: Increasing professional effectiveness.* Boston: Allyn and Bacon.

Notes

Notes

Notes

Notes

Notes

Notes

Notes

Notes

Notes

Notes

Notes

Notes

Notes

Notes

Notes

Notes

Notes

Notes

Notes

Notes